CHRISTIAN PRAYER

CHRISTIAN PRAYER

LADISLAUS BOROS

Translated by David Smith

A CROSSROAD BOOK

The Seabury Press · New York

The Seabury Press
815 Second Avenue
New York, N.Y. 10017

Published originally under the title *Über das christliche Beten*
© 1973 Matthias-Grünewald-Verlag, Mainz, Federal Republic of Germany

English translation © 1976 Search Press Limited

Printed in the United States of America

Library of Congress Cataloging in Publication Data

Boros, Ladislaus, 1927-   Christian prayer.
Translation of Über das christliche Beten.
"A Crossroad book."
1. Prayer.   I. Title.
BV210.2.B6513   1976   248'.3   76-7353
ISBN 0-8164-1199-9

Contents

Foreword

All I say here about prayer is tentative. I try to enter every-day life and look for points of departure. Specialists in the practice of prayer have been too concerned to list duties and methods. I do no more than reveal something of the greatness and the beauty of prayer. At the outset I say quite boldly that prayer is easy, for prayer is not so much an activity as a state of being. We don't have to try very hard. All we have to do is to experience the dynamic power of the Spirit working in us.

I do not want to throw doubt on the great value of "non-Christian" prayer. I am merely looking for an answer to the question: In what sense is prayer an essential part of the Christian way of life?

I do not use the term "Christian prayer" to describe one clearly defined action alongside other activities, but to point to a fundamental attitude on the part of the Christian, which penetrates all his other attitudes. Christian prayer is an openness setting the Christian free to receive God. It is the basic quality of our Christian life.

Modern man is no longer open to God in every respect and in the totality of his experience. He no longer lives in a constant state of closeness to God. He is no longer able to

walk hand in hand with his creator. Man has been plunged
into a life in which God is not standing at every exit. Man
has to break out of this ordinary everyday sphere if he is to
come closer to the God who lives beyond it. That liberating
openness is found in prayer.

But Christian prayer does not simply arise from a basic
human need. It is also a blessing. In prayer, the Christian
opens his whole existence to God who is present everywhere,
but concealed. He shows that he is at the mercy of God in
every aspect of his life. Although it is difficult at first for the
Christian to break out of his day-to-day existence and
become open to God, his prayer will be joyful and easy. What
happens in friendship and in love is very similar. We may
make the effort to be friendly or to love, but ultimately
friendship and love come to us in grace and we receive them
as a gift. Our life as Christians is ultimately a gift which we
accept gratefully.

A Christian lives in this tension of prayer, which is
acquired by his effort and yet accepted as a gift. In the
following pages, then, we shall try to throw light on the
nature of Christian existence so that we may be able to know
why prayer is the necessary foundation of our being as
Christians. Our main concern will not be with theories,
opinions or controversial issues, nor shall we indulge
principally in historical reflection, although these aspects will
be included in different chapters of the book. They are,
however, not central to our quest.

Our task, then, is to demonstrate how the Christian lives
creatively from prayer and enables his existence to be
restored to the state in which God had originally placed it —
a state of closeness to him.

Openness to God

Prayer is a believer's attempt to break out of his ordinary existence in order to become open to God. In his innermost self, he must be open to receive God.

What is that innermost self? In approaching this question, we must be quite honest. In the depths of this self, which ought to be open to God, there are strong instincts and urges, impelling us, on the one hand, to assert ourselves, to speak power and to pursue pleasure and, on the other, leading us to fear, anxiety and disappointment. These hidden depths often seem to be a mere chaos, in which we are no more than a random collection of dark impulses. Does modern man really know himself better than in the past? Sometimes his existence seems to him to be a question mark pointing into the darkness.

To what extent is man, in these dark depths of his existence, capable of prayer? Jesus's answer to this man — and to no other — was: "You ought always to pray and not lose heart". Paul's "Pray constantly" reinforces the Lord's words.

BASIS OF PRAYER

All explicit prayer is founded on the presence of the Spirit in the soul of man. In his letter to the Romans, Paul assures us that the Holy Spirit is praying constantly in the depths of our being, uttering words which we cannot express. It is possible to say that we are constantly praying in our innermost being. All explicit prayer is simply an articulation of that basic state of prayer and this is why we receive an infinitely precious gift of grace every time we become open in prayer to God, even if our prayer is only a hesitant stammering.

We are often conscious of the activity of this basic Christian prayer in us when our hearts are restless and we are carried above and beyond everything that is not divine. At such times, we feel dissatisfied with all we have ever done. At such times too, all that stands between us and God is a paper-thin wall. Occasionally this dividing wall is broken and God himself is suddenly there. He is with us for a while, like Jesus, transfigured, on the way to Emmaus, only to vanish again.

Explicit thought or feeling is often absent from the reality which I have been attempting to describe. From time to time, however, we do think or feel clearly during prayer and when this happens we have in fact entered the sphere of mystical experience. I am convinced that this mystical experience occurs in every Christian who lives a serious life of faith.

I mean simply that mystical prayer is an essential part of Christian life. I do not mean that the Christian always knows explicitly that he is a mystic. But I am sure that a mystical form of grace can be and should be and is active in every Christian at every stage of his basic Christian prayer.

ESSENTIAL PRAYER

The second stage of prayer, which may be called essential prayer, is what happens when we become conscious of the basis of prayer and of the presence of the Holy Spirit in us.

It takes place when we become open to his presence. How can we practise this form of prayer? I think firstly by pausing frequently for a short time during the day, saying nothing and allowing our gaze to rest on God.

We pray essentially when we know that we are secure in the presence of God and rejoice in his nearness. The origins of our life become visible to us in this state and we can hear the waters flowing from the springs of our existence. At the same time, we also have a glimpse of what will be in the future.

Pausing in the midst of life and opening ourselves silently to God should be the basic attitude for all prayer, taking place without strain and in all the different circumstances of everyday existence -- when we are working, studying, relaxing, travelling or conversing. God is always there. He is like the light that shines on everything in the world. He is like the air that we breathe. Suddenly we notice that we no longer need to be induced to pray; God is present and prayer is easy and beautiful. Even our ordinary, everyday lives can be transformed into an essential prayer of this kind.

If we accept our everyday lives as the basis of the eternity that is within us, we shall sooner or later observe that even the least significant things have infinite depth and are heralds of that eternity. In experiencing that reality, Karl Rahner insists again and again, we experience the supernatural and the Holy Spirit is already active within us.

In order to complete the outline of essential prayer – or rather to throw a little more light on what I mean by it – I should like to tell again the story of Our Lady's fool, which is found in a collection of thirteenth-century legends known as the "Lives of the Fathers". A strolling minstrel had spent many years travelling round the world, visiting places both near and far, but was unable to find inner peace. In the end, finding everything and everywhere distasteful, he decided to renounce the worldly life and enter a monastery. The abbot of Clairvaux accepted him as a brother and he was happy for a time. Soon, however, it became clear that he lacked every skill that could be practised in the community. He had never learnt to read, could not recite the Our Father or sing in the choir. He could dance, juggle and entertain, but those were skills which had no place in a monastery.

One day, however, while the brothers were singing in the choir, and he felt very depressed, he went up to the statue of the Virgin Mary and began to speak very humbly. "Blessed Lady," he said, "Body and soul I offer myself to you as your servant. Do not despise my skills. I cannot venerate you, like the other brothers, with prayer and songs of praise, so I will do what the little lambs do in front of their mothers. They leap about and so will I. Look down in mercy on your servant, Lady' "

With this, he began to dance, hopping and jumping gracefully to the right and to the left, both high and low. In this way, the fool served Mary for days on end and his heart was so full of his dancing that he thought of nothing else and wanted to do nothing else. All that he feared was that his secret would be revealed and that he would be driven out of the community and forced to wander again around the world.

One day, the abbot, accompanied by one of the brothers, came to the vault where the statue was and found a hidden place near the altar where they could see without being seen. Very soon the fool arrived and they watched him leaping and dancing until his legs became weak and he fell fainting to the ground. Then, as he lay there, a wonderful figure floated down from the roof, accompanied by a host of angels and archangels, all surrounding the fool and comforting him.

The beautiful Lady then blessed her dancer and, as she floated away, turned her face back towards him again and again.

The abbot and the brother witnessed this scene many times and rejoiced at so great a miracle, but the fool exhausted himself as the years went by until his legs lost their strength and he had to take permanently to bed, mortally ill. When his soul at last left his tired body, our Lady received him in her arms. The angels flew up with his soul — in full sight of the abbot and the monks — to heaven. His body was buried with full honours in the monastery grounds and his grave was visited by pilgrims who thought of it as a holy place.

This legend tells us more than learned treatises about what is meant by "essential prayer". What really constitutes prayer is not words or the way in which it is done, but the fact that it is done by a pure and self-sacrificing heart. If that condition is fulfilled, all doing — even dancing — can become prayer.

VOCAL PRAYER

Silently standing in the presence of God is the second stage of prayer. It is followed, in the normal development of the prayer life, by the third phase, that of vocal prayer, in which, by simply speaking, we confirm and affirm the fact that we are inwardly moved to pray. What we say aloud is of course much less than the experience itself. We express ourselves inadequately when we move from the essential to the vocal stage. Perhaps the most perfect form of vocal prayer is the Jesus prayer, which is found in the Russian *Way of a Pilgrim,* the story of a man who longed to "pray constantly": "Lord Jesus Christ, have mercy on me". This is such a straightforward prayer that even the simplest person can use it, but it is at the same time so profound that it points the way to the great heights of the contemplative life.

A similar prayer that is simple yet deep is the rosary. Nowadays, many Christians dislike it, but that is because they misunderstand it. All that the spoken words of the repeated formulae do is to create, as it were, a holy sphere for us which we enter when we want to pray. This place where we can linger in prayer is in fact always present, but we have to find it and enter it. We can do so by using the material element of the prayer of the rosary, the Hail Marys, when all our spiritual forces are released and we can simply contemplate the figure of Jesus and his life and destiny.

The rosary can in fact become a means of true contemplation. We should not, however, restrict ourselves, in our use of the rosary, to the same set mysteries as in the prayer books. We should feel free to contemplate whatever mysteries in Jesus' life we are moved to contemplate. We may, for example, want to pray: "Jesus, you liked so much to go out with your friends" or "You, who gave back to the poor widow of Naim her only son" or "You, Jesus, created wine from water at the marriage feast at Cana" and to meditate on these freely-chosen mysteries.

We have no need to say explicit, audible prayers at all in order to enter into the presence of God in this way. All that we need are texts taken from the Bible. Three that spring to mind are Mary's song of praise, the *Magnificat*, the prayer of Zechariah, the *Benedictus*, and Simeon's inspired utterance in the Temple, the *Nunc dimittis*, but there are many others equally suitable for vocal prayer: the resurrection of Jesus' friend Lazarus from the dead or the prologue to the gospel of John. Indeed, any passage in Scripture which we find particularly inspiring can be used for this purpose. Texts by and prayers used by especially saintly people are

also very suitable when we pray vocally. They are not difficult to find — they are often contained in collections which
yield great riches to patience and love. In quietly meditating
about these texts and saying them aloud to ourselves, we
learn how to live in a holy community of prayer. Then there
is the one great prayer that Jesus himself has taught us — the
Our Father.

In praying vocally, we should try to pray slowly. We
should pause and breathe deeply every time we begin a word,
a phrase or an exclamation or point for meditation and allow
this to have its full effect on us. If we do this, even the
simplest prayer will open like a flower in full bloom and, in
praying slowly and meditatively in this way, we shall be led
on to the fourth stage of prayer.

CONTEMPLATIVE PRAYER

There are many methods and various aspects of contemplation, but each person has to choose those which suit him best.
Praying contemplatively, he discovers the deep mystery of
even the least significant things. He goes beyond all theories,
opinions, formulae and ideas and begins to understand what
is really meaningful in life. Everything that he has ever
achieved or possessed seems to him to be of no importance
and the only reality that is completely necessary is the
Absolute. Man's inner openness to this Absolute, however,
takes place in an inwardly broken existence, so that doubts,
misgivings and loss of peace are an essential part of the
prayer of contemplation. Contemplative man is bound to
lead his life in a state of uncertainty, but, in the end, all
these many-sided experiences resolve themselves — if contemplation has been practised in the proper way — into a
single togetherness with Christ. If Christ has not been
addressed as "you" during this prayer, the contemplation will

have failed. If, on the other hand, the word "you" has been used with sufficient sincerity and intensity, the person praying contemplatively should then be silent, since he is at last with the Lord.

The aim of contemplation is to develop what has been gained during the previous stages of prayer — basic, essential and vocal prayer — to the full extent of our spiritual powers and to illuminate our own existence in the light of God's. The consequence of this form of prayer should be a total transformation in our ways of thinking, desiring and feeling.

Preparation

This is the most important element in contemplation. If it is at all possible, contemplative prayer should be practised in the morning, even though we are generally more inflexible when we get up than before going to bed, when our thoughts seem to run along of their own accord and often quite lightly and easily. This lightness, however, is deceptive and one has the impression of being impelled forwards towards great depths of experience, although it is really often a case of simply being happy in a harmonious and varied interplay of thoughts and moods. On the other hand, when we pray in the morning and accept the inner poverty of contemplation at this time with fortitude and faithfulness, a true depth of experience may open up within us. We may, in this deep morning contemplation, learn how to pray simply, to persevere in the presence of God and to concentrate on what is essential. Hence it is important to prepare for this morning contemplation in the evening.

A suitable text should be chosen for our evening preparation. This may be an event in the life of Jesus, one of his sayings, addresses or discourses or perhaps a passage from Paul. The content of this text should be set out and analyzed and it may be helpful to select a few key words or themes. Just before going to sleep, we should review our preparation for the contemplation that we intend to practise in the morning, not strenuously or we shall not be able to go to sleep, but gently, perhaps even vaguely and with a sense of anticipation. Our aim should be to weave the truth or the action of Jesus peacefully into the fabric of our sleep, gathering around this holy truth or action that we wish to contemplate all the unconscious forces and images that are alive in our minds. What may then happen is, as Charles Péguy says, that all the individual points of contemplation are thrown together in confusion. When we go to sleep, we all, in fact, become like children: "Nothing is as beautiful, God says, as a child going to sleep while it prays. I tell you, there is nothing as beautiful as this in the world. I have never seen anything more beautiful in the world and yet I have seen many beautiful things. I am quite an expert in beauty and I know nothing more beautiful in the world than a little child falling asleep while praying and the angels smiling as sleep approaches. When this happens, the child confuses everything and understands nothing . . . I have seen the greatest saints, God says, but I tell you, I have never seen anything as amusing and so I know nothing more beautiful in the world . . ."

We should absorb the content of the text for contemplation into our sleep so that it can continue to work quietly and gently within us throughout the night. Then, when morning comes, we can begin the contemplation proper, which should take place – as far as possible – quite peacefully and alongside other tasks. Ignatius of Loyola thought that a quarter of an hour of serious contemplation each day was quite enough for any Christian. It is, however, very important to decide in advance how long the contemplation should last. We should not, when we feel empty, shorten the time that we have resolved to spend in contemplation, nor should we lengthen it when we feel especially spiritual. At the same time, however, we ought, as Christians, to feel quite free in our prayer and we should be careful not to let ourselves be too deeply influenced by the moods and fancies of the moment. Finally, there are four points which are common to all forms of contemplation. The first of these is:

Recollection

We should, both inwardly and outwardly, try to contemplate God in a place where there is no external noise. We should be recollected in God's presence and feel nothing standing between him and ourselves. If this period of recollection is extended until it occupies most of the time that we usually devote to contemplation, we should allow that to happen without anxiety.

Practice

Then the contemplator should read through the biblical text that he has chosen carefully and peacefully and try, especially if the text describes an event in the life of Jesus, to make the scene live in his imagination. He should think of the whole event as if he were there. He should review the action outlined in Scripture, looking for the motives and reasons underlying all that is said and done in the text and clarifying his own attitude towards the events. He should not confine himself to an intellectual examination of the text, but let his emotions be brought into play.

Dialogue

When we have concluded our contemplation, we should be able freely to turn to Christ and to talk about what we have sensed and experienced with him.

Conclusion

The end of our period of contemplation ought to be marked by a concluding prayer, made as slowly and as intensely as possible. If a vocal prayer is preferred at this point, there is no reason why this should not be of our own devising. The Our Father or a simple Amen or sign of the cross may, however, seem a more spontaneous conclusion. This marks the beginning of something else. Our prayer is over and we can leave the sphere of contemplation.

Jesus has taught us the right way of looking at the world. He was the Son of God and knew God better than any living person has ever done. He was the Son of Man and knew the world and men better than any other. He was therefore able to bridge the gulf between the two shores. A Christian's prayer is more than a pious exercise. It joins the world of God and the world of man and thus has cosmic dimensions. When he prays, a Christian celebrates a cosmic liturgy.

PRAYER OF SIMPLICITY

If contemplation is practised appropriately, it always tends to become simpler. As our ideas, thoughts and feelings diminish in number, their depth and intensity increase. This is the fifth stage of prayer and can best be called the prayer of simplicity. The more deeply we experience God as the one who cannot be thought of in ideas or expressed in words, the more we are able to bring our prayer down to the basic level of persisting in silence.

This silence is the highest form of prayerful existence, in which man sums up the whole of his life in the simple word Yes. Man's openness to the finality of things is marked by his silence in the face of the ultimate mystery, a silence broken from time to time when this affirmation is expressed fervently, but so gently that it can scarcely be heard. This word Yes anticipates what man will say at the moment of his death and contains the germ of his eternal life. In mystical theology, God is often called the nameless one and, apart from this, all that can be said is not about God himself, but about man's persistent waiting for and hoping in him. But this waiting and this hoping point to the true significance of the namelessness of God, since, in this extremely simple form of prayer, man's whole exstence is concentrated on one point of expectation and intersection. This point has several names in mystical theology, all of which indicate the same fundamental reality — the summit, the centre or the ground of the soul.

MYSTICAL PRAYER

A Christian as such — and man precisely as man — does not realize his destiny or reach fulfilment until he enters the mystical reality. Man who is, as it were, not mystical, is living a purely illusory existence in a world of appearances. Mysticism is in no sense a flight from ideas and images. On the contrary, it transforms them, to such an extent that it is possible to claim that mystical knowledge is the perfection of knowledge as such. Mysticism can be defined as the experiential union with God and this definition has the merit not only of being logically consistent with what we have just said, but also of being completely self-evident. Mystical prayer is therefore not really a further step in the practice of prayer — mystical experience can occur at any of the individual stages of prayer that we have outlined in this chapter, although there is a special form of mysticism which is peculiar to each age of man, the most distinctive of which is perhaps the mystical experience of childhood.

Mysticism is ultimately the transformation of man's whole view of the world. Ordinary man almost unquestioningly accepts matter and material existence as the final reality of being. For a mystic, on the other hand, the spiritual reality is true being. In a balanced state of mysticism, man is in complete harmony with the world and with himself. Mysticism is the perfection of man's being.

When a Christian prays he is letting himself, in the midst of the stresses of his life on earth, be refashioned by God's way of thinking and acting, by God's very being. That makes a Christian stronger than the world in the depths of his own suffering.

Basic elements

The best of all norms to measure prayer is absence of intention. At first, that may seem a very surprising choice, since man's existence almost always consists of a closely woven fabric of intentions. He does not, as a rule, simply make himself available to his fellow men. He always seems to be wanting something: he wants to make an impression on others, wants them to envy him, wants to gain an advantage over them or wants to get ahead at their expense. Only very seldom are men able to co-exist in free and equal relationships with each other. Most human relationships are built up on the basis of dependence or intention: on advantage.

But there is another, radically different, kind of inter-personal relationship, based on an open encounter between a man and his fellow men. This type of relationship changes inevitably for the worse or ceases to exist as soon as the attitude of one or more of those involved in it is determined by intention. If the relationship, however, is conducted at the true personal level of "I" and "you", then the partners will want nothing from each other and all intention is bound to wither away.

It is only possible for man to exist together with his fellow men at a truly human level in the absence of all intention.

When this condition is fulfilled, there will be true friendship and love and men will really help each other in their need without even thinking of a reward.

The Christian saint is fundamentally a man whose false self has been overcome, and who therefore no longer sees everything in terms of his own success or power over others. In him, the truth has been set free. He is present in the world, but does not have to draw attention to his presence. He is powerful, but does not have to exert himself. He is without fear. If he is entirely without intention, man is open to God. He becomes the "door" through which God's power is able to flow into the world. He is not simply turned towards himself in his actions. He does not seek his own advantage, nor does he wish merely to assert himself over others. He is, on the contrary, entirely turned towards others.

That is the underlying meaning of the mystery of God's creative activity. God created us without any intention at all and purely because he rejoiced in our being. In the same way, he has no intention in his leading of the history of the world to its ultimate fulfilment. His providence, by which he guides the world towards its end, is entirely lacking in intention and is, in fact, divine wisdom in its purest form. It is by ths wisdom of God that the whole complex structure of the world is held together. Because God's wisdom prevails, things are not simply a confusion of isolated events and actions and our world continues to be a meaningful and closely-knit unity.

If we apply the norm of this absence of intention to the practice of Christian prayer, we find that four basic elements of prayer emerge: adoration, praise, thanksgiving and petition.

ADORATION
In adoration, man bows down before the greatness of God,

and begins to sense the real meaning of the word "God." God, he feels, simply is and can never not be; he is life, love and truth. If the world ceased to be, nothing essential would be lacking— God would be and that would be enough.

As soon as we humbly accept the fact that we are created, a new world is revealed to us. We begin to see that everything exists as the image and form of God himself. We begin to understand that we carry within us the brightness of the Deity, simply because we have been created, and that, because of this brightness, we also carry within us the worthiness of God. Adoration means not simply bowing down before the greatness of God, but freely placing ourselves at his mercy.

Adoration is of fundamental importance bcause it acts as a guarantee of our spiritual health. But how does our spirit become sick? Romano Guardini said: "What is usually known as a sickness of the spirit is really a sickness of the nerves or of the mind. A sickness of the spirit as such can only occur if what underlies the health of the spirit breaks down. Spiritual health is based on truth and justice and the spirit becomes sick when it departs from the truth". Guardini then asks: "What has all this to do with adoration?" and replies: "It has everything to do with adoration, because the man who adores God can never experience a complete spiritual disorder. Both in his inner attitude and, when it comes to the point, in the actions that he performs in the outside world, the man who worships God will always be preserved in the truth. However often he may say or do the wrong thing, however frequently he may deeply be shaken, the fundamental order and direction of his existence will remain undisturbed".

The Bible is full of the theme of adoration. When Ezekiel saw the glory of the Lord, he fell down upon his face (Ezek.

1. 28), like Saul when the risen Lord appeared to him on the road to Damascus (Acts 9. 4). This attitude of adoration is expressed in the Old Testament above all in two symbolic actions — throwing oneself down and kissing. God is the power and the glory, exalted as a ruler above everything (1 Chron. 29. 11), and all peoples are therefore bound to throw themselves down before him (Ps 99. 1-5) and all the earth has to worship him (Ps 96.9). Kissing expresses belonging together and love. The whole of man's attitude towards God is summarized in a very striking way in the closely connected actions of falling down before God and kissing. They point to the fact that we are separated from God by a great abyss, but that we at the same time feel powerfully drawn to him.

This attitude of worship is perfected under the New Covenant. We are told in John 4. 24 that "those who worship him must worship in spirit and truth". In this adoration, the whole man, "spirit and soul and body" (1 Thess. 5. 23), is dedicated to God. According to the fourth gospel (John 4. 20-23), the Christian has no need, because he is totally dedicated to God, to go to a particular place, such as Jerusalem, in order to adore God. Everything belongs to the Christian, because he is Christ's and Christ is God's (1 Cor. 3. 23).

The classical position of adoration or worship, both in the catacombs and in the liturgy, is to stand with outstretched arms. This posture represents the person who is caught up in and carried away by longing for God, and yet discreetly reserved in the presence of his Lord.

PRAISE

In Scripture, God's greatness has the character of glory. This means that the reality of God is radiant. In the presence of this radiance, adoration is transformed into the joy of praise. When we praise God, we think above all of God himself and not so much of his gifts, as we may do in thanksgiving. Praise is more theocentric than thanksgiving. It is more absorbed in God and closer to adoration.

The two outstanding examples of songs of praise in the New Testament are Mary's (the Magnificat, Luke 1. 46-55) and Zechariah's (the Benedictus, Luke 1. 58-79). The Church's liturgy too has always relied to a great extent on such songs of praise, hymns and sequences as the famous Te Deum, as well as the psalms of Israel. Sometimes, it would seem, man's praise of God goes out to embrace the whole world and all the things of creation.

Praise of God characterizes all created beings, but how can we fulfil what God so earnestly desires and respond fully to our divine vocation to live for the praise of God's glory? That question has been answered by the mystic Elizabeth of the Trinity, who distinguished four ways of praising God.

Absolute priority

"A perfect praise of God's glory is the soul which rests in God and loves him with a pure and selfless love without seeking itself in the enjoyment of this love. The soul which loves and praises God in this way no longer loves him for his gifts even if it receives nothing more from him."

Perfect readiness

"A perfect praise of God's glory is the soul which waits, like a harp, in quiet recollection, ready to receive the mysterious touch of the Holy Spirit which will release the divine melody. Such a soul knows that suffering itself is a string from which even more beautiful sounds can come and is therefore glad when these sounds are found on its instrument, because the heart of God may be touched all the more delicately".

Power to assimilate
"A perfect praise of God's glory is the soul which is fixed unwaveringly on God in the simplcty of faith. Such a soul is like a mirror reflecting God's very being, like an unfathomable abyss into which God can flow or like a crystal which can be filled with God's rays."

Promptness in thanksgiving
"A perfect praise of God's glory is the soul which is constantly thanking God. Every one of its thoughts, impulses and actions, indeed, the whole of its being plunge it deeper and deeper into the love of God and at the same time ring out like an echo of the sanctus resounding from the depths of eternity."

Here is a summary of the essential teaching of mystical theology. Thanksgiving appears under the heading of praise. This shows how fluid the borderline in fact is between the individual elements of Christian prayer. It also shows – and this may be even more important – that thanksgiving does not necessarily follow a petition that has been heard and answered (as it clearly ought to), but that everything is already within us as a gift from God for which we have to give thanks without having asked for it. We ought also to thank God for the fact that he is and that he is as he is. We ought to thank him for our redemption, for the Church, for our own life and destiny and for much more besides. We can therefore with confidence call the third element in prayer:

THANKSGIVING
Understood in this sense, thanksgiving is fundamentally man's positive reaction to God's love. When we want to

emphasize the depths to which man's spirit can penetrate, we often use the word "devotion" and it is clear too that giving thanks is very close indeed to praising, glorifying and exalting God. Just as no one can accurately define where faith ceases and hope and love begin, so too is it impossible for any one of us to say with certainty where praise ends and thanksgiving begins.

Man does not come from himself, but from God. The whole of creation has God as its origin and man is part of that whole. All existence is therefore the recipient of a superabundance of grace, and man, who is directly affected by this grace, can only respond by giving thanks. All of us have, at some time or other in our lives, experienced the need to thank another person simply because he is. We want to thank him not because he has done something for us or for someone we know, but just for being. This feeling of thankfulness for a person's being may also occur in our relationship with God and when we thank him simply for being what he is our thanksgiving has a deep and mysterious significance: "We give you thanks for your great glory".

God's inexpressible being contains something mysterious: a quality that can be called the "freedom of real being". It is as though God's being were itself a grace that he grants to us, a power for which man is compelled to give thanks.

If it is borne up by faith, our thanksgiving can certainly be extended to include what is difficult and, if it is successful, our whole existence can be transformed. A Christian has to learn how to give thanks and indeed to learn it again and again. He has to reject the kind of indifference which makes him take everything that happens for granted. He should not accept the events of daily life as a matter of course and should therefore begin by including precisely these ordinary things in thanksgiving. In the morning, when we still feel fresh and pure after our night's rest, we should say to God: "Thank you God that I am here and that I am breathing. I thank you for everything that I have and for everything that exists around me". When we have eaten, we ought to thank God for our food and then, at night, we ought to give thanks again. "Thank you, God," we could say, "for letting me live, work and be happy today. Thank you for letting me meet this person and be made aware of the goodness and faithfulness of another. You have given me all that I have experienced today and I thank you for it".

PETITION

Questions are often asked about the holy, yet perfectly natural character of petition. One of the most frequent is: why is it sometimes so difficult, even impossible, for us to ask God?

Pride may be a great obstacle to petitionary prayer. The proud man will not ask because he despises his and others' humanity. But, on the other hand, even sin has not completely extinguished the spark of worthiness that God has lit in every man, with the result that our request is in itself worthy and, when it is granted, this too is a worthy action. We are entirely dependent on God's grace. If we admit this and make the reality our own, we shall become more humble.

A second difficulty is God's apparent weakness in the world. Everything in the world seems to happen as it is bound to happen and there seems to be no room any more for a God who can help man and gives to him. But, just as he has, in the case of pride, to learn a simple but fundamental lesson over again, so must a man recognize that the events that take place in the world are not entirely self-enclosed, but happen inside a man. The value of each event depends on a man's attitude. Applying this principle to petitionary prayer, we find that to ask is fundamentally to receive already, since our asking makes it possible for us to see the events in the context of God's power. If, then, we change our attitude, we shall be able to accept that God is certainly never too weak to help us to change in this way.

A third difficulty that is often encountered in connection with asking God is that we have the feeling that he is unreal. He is, we sometimes think, a pious thought, but he is not able to stand up to the harsh reality of the world. In thinking this, of course, we are forgetting how great God in fact is. He has, after all, created the world and so does not enter into competition with it.

The indifference of God is an impression which modern man very often has, making it difficult or impossible for him to ask God for anything. God simply does not seem to be concerned with or for the world. On the one hand, there is man living in this world and he can find no way out of his enclosed, suffering existence. On the other, there is God in his own world and there is no point of contact between them. This fourth difficulty is frequently encountered by those often quiet, retiring people for whom life has contained a great deal of bitter experience and everything always seems to turn out badly. A Christian's task is quite clearly revealed here — he has, as it were, to make up for God's deficiency by kindling the fire of his love in a world that has grown cold and by making God smile at others and enlighten the dark lives of men. Those people who think that God is indifferent to them and their world very much need to encounter human love and friendship.

There is a fifth difficulty which is perhaps the greatest of all — that God is disappointing. How often one hears it said — and not always by the worst people! -- that God does not listen to or answer prayer. We must wait for his prayer to be heard, and the answer may perhaps be found in a place that is quite different from the one in which we were looking.

The New Testament says: "But when you pray, go into your room and shut the door and pray to your Father who is in secret: and your Father who sees in secret will reward you. And in praying do not heap up empty phrases as the gentiles do; for they think that they will be heard for their many words. Do not be like them, for your Father knows what you need before you ask him" (Matt. 6. 6–8). What do these well-known words from the Sermon on the Mount mean? I think they mean that, when we pray, we should do it as a matter of course, so that it contains no trace of self-enjoyment or hypocrisy. The room is symbolic and the implied contrast is with the street, where we act publicly in front of other people. Then we are told that we should not use too many words when we pray. Pray but at the same time recognise that God knows better than you do what you need. If you pray in the light of this knowledge, you will be praying in the way in which Christ intends you to pray. Finally, God knows what your words will be even before you pronounce them, yet you should still pray. In everything that you do, say and think, you are known to God.

Mark 11. 24 says: "Whatever you ask in prayer, believe that you receive it, and you will". This points to the certainty in faith that is attached to the prayer of petition and is so constructed that three different tenses are used in the one short sentence describing the certainty that the Christian's request made in prayer will be granted. The first verbs, "ask and pray" are in the present, the verb "receive" is in the past and the last verb, "to be", is in the future. The second phrase, which is literally "believe that you have received", is often made weaker in translation by being rendered as "that you will receive it" or simply, as in the Revised Standard

Version above, "that you receive it". If we are to interpret Mark 11. 24 correctly, however, we should preserve the tenses of the original text. This means that the passage will read: "Whatever you pray and ask for, believe that you have received and it will be (given) to you".

In this form, it contains a clear echo of the word of the Lord as expressed by the prophet Isaiah: "Before they call, I will answer them" (Is. 65.24). It also bears a striking resemblance to the sentence from the Sermon on the Mount: "Your Father knows what you need before you ask him" (Matt. 6. 8). These words of Jesus are certainly in line with the whole tradition of the gospels, according to which Jesus spent hours, often at night, in lonely, urgent prayer of petition. There is a certain kind of prayer which is always heard by God under all circumstances. This is the petition which can best be expressed in the formula: "Thy will be done in my life".

In this petition, what we want coincides with what God himself wants. In asking God in this way, we are really sharing in his providence.

We should be spurred on to ask God again and again, since the Christian prayer of petition contains an inspiring truth. It is a trustful recognition of God's adorable providence. As soon as this truth is grasped, all sense of disappointment in God's apparent failure to listen to us when we ask will disappear. Our most urgent and profound request is, after all, not to be helped to achieve some individual aim. It is to be given the grace to enable us to be inwardly transformed so that we shall be able to see the true meaning of life with new eyes.

But what should we ask for and how are we to know that God really hears us? I can give no ready answer except to say that we should not try to minimize the difficulty of the prayer of petition, because it can lead to a deep insight into the nature of God, the nature of the world and the nature of man. All three are given a more profound meaning as soon as we begin to reflect about providence. It is not easy in the modern age to believe in God's providence, not in spite of the difficulties of petitionary prayer, but on account of them. But it may be our only solution.

Good intention

A good intention is not a special virtue of weak Christians, but it can provide them with consolation. It is not a flight from our task in the world, but it can provide salvation for the one who is in flight. It is not a justification for failure in the world, but it can in many cases justify failure. To have a good intention is to be orientated towards a good end, but to be, as it were, indifferent whether we achieve our aim or whether we shall benefit from it. A distinction has to be made between our intention and success. What ultimately counts in Christian life is our inner attitude: the intention that we have in mind when we perform our everyday, often humdrum duties. What takes place in this attitude is the prayer of our whole Christian being; the effects produced by our being in the world are, by comparison, unimportant. There is a well-known saying: The road to hell is paved with good intentions. In my definition of "good intention", that saying is not true.

VIRTUE OF THE STRONG
By "strong", I mean an inner superiority to the world and to the events in the world. The man who is superior in this way has a good conscience and can accept the events that occur in

the world, assess their value and adopt a correct attitude towards them. This implies that the person who stands up for the truth will also stand up for God. At the same time, it is also important to realize that the truth is often in a position of weakness in the world and is therefore open to any attack. If this truth is to result in virtue, then, two further factors must be added — on the one hand, we must have consideration for the person who hears the truth and, on the other, we must have courage if what is said is not easy to grasp. Truthfulness is a virtue, not of the weak, but of those who are inwardly strong and who can be both considerate to others and at the same time courageous. The person who combines in himself and expresses both consideration and courage is obviously someone who has a "good intention".

It is, however, not only in truthfulness that this tension between consideration for others and courage can be found. It can also be discovered in other virtues — in goodness, understanding, thankfulness and recollection, for example. I have only chosen truthfulness as one example among many and what I have particularly in mind is its biblical meaning, as expressed, for instance, in Paul's text: "speaking the truth in love" (Eph. 4. 15). My aim is above all firstly to reveal the inner tenderness that is always present in those who are really strong and secondly to point to the damage that has been done to this virtue especially in the present age. To have a good intention is to be well-disposed towards other people and indeed towards all creation.

CONSOLATION FOR THE WEAK

What about those Christians who can be called "weak"? We know, after all, that it was above all for them that Christ brought redemption and that there is no one who is completely strong. We are all, in one way or another, weak. How can our weakness be transformed, in prayer, into a virtue? I think that that can only be done by means of a "good intention"

We have all failed at some time, perhaps many times, in our lives in friendship, in love or in carrying out our duty. Even the apostles withdrew after Christ's ascension. Out of fear of pursuit, they behaved like cowards. In their hearts, however, they were expecting the fulfilment of a promise. God came to these poor, frightened men above all because it was only human weakness which made them afraid – their inner attitude was fundamentally correct. Their intention was, in other words, good. However afraid they were of arrest, they stayed together as a community of believers and "with one accord devoted themselves to prayer" (Acts 1. 14). They were frightened and anxious, yes, but together they hoped in God and persisted in prayer. This gave them courage and consolation. In the same way, the hope of all the weak followers of Christ will be fulfilled.

FLIGHT FROM THE WORLD

To have a good intention is basically to be in agreement with God. This comes about when man's inner state of readiness and alertness is completely in tune with whatever demand God makes of him at any moment. We decide to accomplish what is good in this particular situation.

In making this decision, an individual Christian is in fact saying: I stand alone in this. I have to answer for this decision and no one else can be held responsible for it. No one else can take the responsibility for this choice from me and this is what constitutes my dignity as a human being. My conscience as a human individual is the basis of my greatness because it enables me to perceive and to accomplish something which did not exist previously.

Everything — the things and events of this world and the very substance of life itself — forms the material of this attitude. Goodness is not simply a dead law. It is infinite life, striving to enter the reality of day to day existence and to achieve a human form in this world. The attempt to do good in everyday life is certainly not just a question of carrying out a precept. It is much more than this. It is, in the deepest sense of the word, a creative activity in which something which did not exist in the world before is brought into being. The Christian who does good, then, has the task of giving a human shape to what is infinite and eternal.

This has two consequences. The first is that we can grasp this great, eternal reality of goodness that calls to be made real in the world here and now. We are able to grasp it with the essential freedom not only of our human will, but also of our innermost heart and declare that we are quite ready to do good. This full consent takes place deep within us and our inner life becomes open and receptive "until it is all leavened" (Matt. 13. 33).

Our good intention is not something special existing alongside other realities. Everything that exists forms its content, with the result that the whole of reality has to be envisaged if our good intention is to be made true within it. A Christian is called upon to seek, to think and to exchange ideas in carrying out his good intention, but the most important aspect of all is that he should become aware of his actual task in the world now.

The second consequence is that we are able to understand the reality of goodness in the light of our situation here. If our good intention is not closely related to this real situation, it will never be more than a fruitless desire.

FAR FROM SIMPLE
The more alert one is to the demands made by people, things and relationships, the more difficult it is to know what to do. In the formation of man's conscience, his horizon is made wider and he is made more sensitive to the multiplicity of values and claims that exist in the world. But, as his conscience becomes more fully formed and his openness and sensitivity are increased, there is a growing danger that he will lose himself in this multiplicity and that he will be so preoccupied with seeing, understanding and the desire to do things properly that he will never be able to make a clear decision and act. If he is to overcome this fundamental difficulty and carry out his good intention, man – and above all the man who wants to do what is right in the world – needs to contemplate and to weigh relationships against each other in the presence of God.

EVERY SITUATION IS UNIQUE
Each of our good intentions has to be made incarnate in a given situation and each of these situations is new and will probably never recur.

WE DO NOT ALWAYS WANT WHAT IS GOOD
Romano Guardini says: "We often resist doing what is good . . . (An evil intention) influences not only what we do, but also our power of recognition and judgment. It draws our mind away from the object. It emphasizes certain aspects of the object or else tones them down. It throws light on some features and obscures others. It distorts and can even cause the object to disappear entirely. It is clear from this experience what has to be done by the human conscience in such cases. The man whose conscience is alert will be open to the whole of the situation confronting him. He will see the

people involved as they are. He will weigh up the various relationships and bear in mind all the different demands made by the situation, which he will contemplate with eyes untroubled by inhibiting or diverting factors. He will penetrate more and more deeply into the heart of the situation, aided by his purified conscience. He will be able to see because he really wants to see".

If the situation is open to many different interpretations and it is not at all clear in which direction the right action lies, the only possible way of coming to a decision is by allowing our good intention to take over. We must simply say, it is bound to happen in this way and this is in any case the best solution. Our attitude will include obedience and a willingness to create anew, understanding and judgment, an attempt to penetrate to the heart of the matter and, finally, decision. And there is surely no other way for this attitude to come about apart from contemplative prayer.

SALVATION FOR THE ESCAPER

We are impelled by our good intention to accomplish the will of God in the situation in which we find ourselves. What are we to do if we cannot make the infinite goodness of God present in our world? How can we justify our flight from God? If we approached the task without a good intention and then failed, then all that we can do is to ask God to forgive us and he most certainly will. But what should we do if we really undertook the task with a good intention?

Man is often simply tired. Sometimes he just goes about things in the wrong way. He often simply does not recognize a difficulty when it approaches and cannot take up the right attitude towards it. He may be incapable of analyzing the reasons underlying the problem or of finding a suitable solution. The result is that he fails in this particular task. Does that mean that he is a bad man?

We all have the experience, almost every day of our lives, of trying to do something that is not only undeniably right, but also good. We want, for instance, to help someone out of a state of spiritual confusion. To begin with, everything seems to go all right. Everything fits neatly into everything else and the good work that we have performed gives an impression of beauty and perfection. We feel a sense of deep thankfulness and humility. Then, at another time with the same person or with someone else, everything goes wrong. We say the same things, but perhaps we fail to express that deep commitment which previously made what we said so convincing and what we did such a powerful testimony. The result is disappointing and all that remains for us to do is to take our experience to a psychiatrist, who will perhaps succeed in levelling out our personality so that we may in the end no longer be an "object" influenced by good or by evil.

It is, however, possible that God may not want us to succeed in everything. He only wants our intention to be good and our effort to be sincere. If we try, then, and in spite of everything do not accomplish anything, we certainly have an excuse — not a pretext, but a genuine excuse. Our intention was good and, on both the first and the second occasion in the example given above, we behaved honestly and openly towards the other person. In the first case, we succeeded but, in the second, we failed. The whole question is ultimately in God's hands and he will find a way of contrasting our failure with his power and even perhaps of drawing from our failure some greater good. In cases such as this, we have above all to seek an inner composure and recollectedness. It is necessary to have led a life of prayer in order to recognize God's goodness and generosity and to be able to say: it doesn't matter.

NOT A JUSTIFICATION OF FAILURE

Christians are sometimes criticized for having defended the doctrine of the "good intention" in order to protect themselves against the possibility of their own failure. This is not true. What has constantly to be borne in mind is that man lives in a state of inner confusion. His highest powers — those of the spirit, mind, heart and desire — are inwardly confused. It is therefore worth remembering that Jesus revealed himself as "the way" (John 14. 6). The man who does not rely on his own powers, then, will undoubtedly be crowned with success in the world, but this success must be accepted in the spirit of Christ himself — in humility.

A text which is most relevant in the context of this question is the ancient hymn on the humiliation and exaltation of the Son of God that is found in Paul's letter to the Philippians: "Do nothing from selfishness or conceit, but in humility count others better than yourselves. Let each of you look not only to his own interests, but also to the interests of others. Have this mind among yourselves, which you have in Christ Jesus, who, though he was born in the form of God, did not count equality with God a thing to be grasped, but emptied himself, taking the form of a servant, being born in the likeness of men. And being found in human form he humbled himself and became obedient unto death, even death on a cross. Therefore God has highly exalted him and bestowed on him the name which is above every name, that at the name of Jesus every knee should bow, in heaven and on earth, and every tongue confess that Jesus Christ is Lord, to the glory of God the Father" (Phil. 2. 3–11).

The Son of God did not cling forcefully and at the same time anxiously to his eternal being as though it were something that had been wrongly appropriated. On the contrary, he emptied himself, making himself a slave. So serious was this act of self-destruction that it went as far as death, even death on a cross. From this, however, came his new name, the name of the Christ, the victorious, anointed one, the Kyrios or Lord God who reigns in glory over all creation.

It is a very strange mystery that success should be achieved in an act of self-emptying. Yet if a man really wants to achieve success in friendship and love, in his own thoughts and knowledge and in his own desires, he must empty himself. There is no other way for him to become really man. If he is to do that with complete sincerity, he must have a pure conscience and a good intention. If he has that attitude and regards it as the fulfilment of his human nature, he will be bearing genuine Christian witness in the world. Once again, however, this witness can only be borne as the result of prayer.

JUSTIFYING FAILURE

What are we to do if the tension between self-emptying and perfection, as described above, does not exist and if our lives as Christians are simply not equal to the demands made by Christ? What will be the situation if our faith is not strong enough? If we fail in regard to God himself? If we lack faith? If our failure reaches as far as the ultimate mystery of life itself? How shall we be placed if we find that the truths of Christ's revelation appear to lose their meaning for us?

Any of these questions can give rise to deep conflicts and everything will ultimately depend on whether or not we are really serious about our faith in God. We should not force ourselves to believe in the truths of revelation when faith seems almost impossible. But we ought not to abandon faith entirely because we are experiencing serious difficulties or are fighting a losing battle with certain aspects. What would be a good intention, in a situation of that kind, in which we find ourselves close to inner failure? I think it would testify to a good intention if we were to say to ourselves: The truth can take time.

There is a great diversity of faith in the Church. I understand and admire the attitude of many Christians, who accept in principle the essential teachings of the Christian Church, even though they may not yet have reached the point (who among us has?) where they are able to make all these truths of faith existentially their own. Clearly, there is no question here of postponing a radical decision. It is simply the normal human phenomenon of allowing ourselves and others the time to become mature, in this case, in matters of faith.

God is patient with man and has always been so throughout human history. He has always waited for his truth to grow in man and bear fruit. Christian teaching is above all not a collection of individual truths, all of which have to be inculcated with equal insistence or which we have to make equally our own before we can begin to live according to the one truth. I would rather describe Christianity as a doorway in the world's being leading from many different individual truths — even errors — into the one truth. No one should be obliged or persuaded to grasp the whole of faith at one time. We must recognise that it is often not possible to answer many questions concerning faith, including those of ultimate importance, and that these may frequently have to remain open for a long time.

Such people have a legitimate place in the Christian Church. Other Christians who have fully appropriated all the truth of the Church — if there are any such others — have a duty to accept and welcome these questioning believers in friendship as their brothers and sisters in Christ. All are looking together, in history, for God and for an understanding of his mystery.

Another, closely related question is often overlooked in the Christian's life of prayer. Living faith is not simply a fixed, unchanging knowledge, a skill which is there for the whole of our lives, whatever happens to us. It is not like a "times table" that we learned when we were young and still know and can recite whether life is going well or badly.

Faith is not like that because it is intimately bound up with and affected by the whole of our existence. Since we as men often experience uncertainty and helplessness in our daily lives, our faith is also again and again made uncertain and helpless. There are many reasons for this. Our inner resources may be exhausted. We may be approaching a new time of life. We may be entering an entirely new environment or moving among quite different people. All these factors will influence us and may disturb us. They are, however, fundamentally natural and should be accepted as such. Faith is, after all, not something self-enclosed, but rather a reality which is, as we have said, closely connected with our lives. It is, however, more than this. It is inseparably tied not only to man, but also to God, who reveals himself to man. Our feeling about faith, then, may change or even disappear altogether, but this close connexion remains and it would be true to say that the essence of faith is to be found in our perseverance.

I am very glad that there are so many Christians who go about spreading peace and happiness and see things in their right proportions. These men and women are balanced and positive enough to show, by their attitude to life and faith, that there is no cause for anyone to think in terms of catastrophe and disaster in the Church. Most members of the Church find such people a source of quiet inspiration, in whose company they can breathe freely because they are on neither side. They form the third force in the Church. This type of wise, discreet Christian has, of course, always been present in the Church. They are the real peace-makers among us and wherever they are they bring order where disorder existed. Their function is very humble and soon forgotten. Quite often, others claim recognition for what these people have done. But what does it matter? With their serenity, recollectedness, complete absence of hostility and concentration on what is essential in the gospel message, they play an indispensable part in purifying the whole atmosphere in the Church.

I have tried to show, by discussing in some detail three sets of facts which seem to be mutually contradictory, how a "good intention" can produce beneficial and positive effects in our everyday lives. A good intention characterizes strong Christians, but it can also bring consolation to the weak. It is the attitude of those who carry out their Christian task in the world, but it also provides salvation for those who are in flight from the world. Although success is always marked by good intention, it can also be a justification for those who fail.

It is possible for what we call unhappiness — a serious loss or illness, for example — to become a cause of great happiness. This will happen, however, only on condition that we see this unhappy experience in the light of faith and treat it positively as a good intention. A good intention may give all that we do for God and our fellow men the purity that is necessary if we are to do anything in an authentic Christian spirit. Our good intention is fundamentally no more than an expression of our purity of heart.

Repentance

Man is not completely at the mercy of his past. What he has already become can be and is transformed in such a way that he changes his past into a future. This transformation of the past does not take place automatically. Man has to decide for himself what of the past he will take with him into the future. This means that he will have to say No many times, to what he has become. I shall try to show how and why this No to the past can and ought to be a prayer.

Almost all the outstanding figures in the history of religion have had the painful experience of reviewing their past lives in this way. The call to conversion and repentance echoes throughout the whole of the Old Testament and the New Testament opens in the same way with a call to man to become entirely different. This is an essential characteristic of prayer, since all authentically human and Christian life is led within the context of repentance, of our being set free from our own guilty past. Good and evil have to be separated from each other in our lives.

In this chapter, my aim is merely to show what is really meant by repentance and especially repentance as prayer.

SORROW

The first stage in being set free from the past can be called sorrow or regret. If it is to be properly understood, we must consider how man has become what he is and how his destiny is built up of many parts. Man is formed by his own actions. He is changed by every good or bad action that he performs and his past continues to live within him, either giving him a firm foothold on life or else filling his present existence with poison. Man also exists at several different levels at the same time.

At the biological level, it is clear that man has little freedom. He is formed by a concentration of biological factors which reach far back into the obscurity of the past. His biological origins go back thousands of millions of years into prehuman history.

In the psychological sphere too, man is also powerfully over-shadowed by the past. Although what he has experienced in the past may be transformed, it can — especially if it is unfavourable — disturb the life of the spirit in the present. There is also a continued existence, in this intermediate sphere of man's psychological life, not only of personal, but of primordial experiences.

In addition to these there is a third level: that of "objective spirit". This objective spirit is the basis of man's spiritual life and is that part of it which is not dependent on the subject. Individual thinking and choice are always part of communal reflection and selection and this in turn belongs to the greater cultural environment. The particular cultural environment is deeply embedded in the whole of mankind's experience itself. Man is therefore rooted in the past in a way which is difficult, perhaps impossible for us to establish precisely at present.

The most specifically human aspect of the individual is

his personal being. As a person, he is completely dependent on himself alone and can rise above what he has become. He can pass judgment on himself and even turn against himself. In this very special sphere of his being, the personal sphere, he can freely create himself and set himself free from his past. He can say No to what he has become and be sorry for it.

What is this sorrow? It is possible for man to cause his past to cease to exist? Sorrow is undoubtedly helpful because it enables man to see that he can stand at a distance from himself. In sorrow, he can say: My own misery is known to me, but although I fall short of the ideal, I long for an end that is better and greater. I am sorry that I have not become something quite different.

This honest examination is one of our most important tasks when we pray. A word that may help us to understand this task is "recollection", because it points clearly to the victory of honesty at the level of the human soul. This essential state of serenity in the soul is often the fruit of a long period of testing in life.

SHAME

In shame, I can say quite honestly: If it is really my destiny to be with others in the world, I ought to be a light shining for those others. But I am not. I ought to give myself, just as I am, just as I have become, to them in love. But I do not. In the very act of giving myself, I hold myself back. This act of humility calls for total selflessness, which can be achieved only in prayer. Two biblical examples may enable us to understand the part played in this by shame, the betrayal of Jesus by Judas Iscariot and his betrayal by Peter. Both these men tried to overcome their shameful past.

Judas, we are told, after betraying Jesus, "went and hanged himself" (Matt. 27. 5). We should not, however, judge him too hastily, but remember that he was driven to do this out of shame. This at least shows that he had a certain inner greatness and that he could not bear to go on living in shame as a traitor. On the other hand, he interpreted his guilty past purely as guilt and this interpretation was final and definitive. By ending his life, he eliminated the possibility that his betrayal of Jesus might have had another, more positive meaning. His betrayal could therefore never become anything other than a pure act of treachery.

That is not a judgement on Judas' eternal fate. It is simply our interpretation of his life as led on this earth, insofar as we are acquainted with it. In this context, I should like to ask a personal, but relevant question. Are we all perhaps not guilty of doing the same as those other "Christians" who are convinced that they are justified when they pass judgment on Judas and condemn him to eternal damnation? Surely no one is justified in this conviction − after all, to the very end Jesus persisted in calling Judas his friend. And what two friends have to say to each other at the end concerns them alone. None of us is in any way justified in feeling superior to Judas. In one way or another, each of us has at some time betrayed Jesus. All that we have to do is to ask him, as our Lord, to go on calling us his friend until the end. That may be much more than we ought to expect him to do for us.

Peter betrayed Jesus, but his reaction was quite different from Judas's. We are told by the evangelist that "he went out and wept bitterly" (Matt. 26. 75). His betrayal was an evil action, but for him it became a stage on the way of the cross of his own life and led him ultimately to happiness and holiness. There is no more striking example in the Bible of the way in which the past can be given an entirely new value, provided that man is prepared, in spite of everything, to make a new beginning and to open himself without reservation in love, in other words, to say honestly: "Yes, Lord, you know that I love you" (John 21. 15,16,17).

We should not forget that Jesus was testing Peter severely — his three questions, "Do you love me?", correspond to Peter's three-fold denial in the courtyard, while Jesus was being tried. As we have seen in the case of Judas, no one is ever rejected in advance. On the other hand, no one receives salvation purely by chance, without repentance.

This is the point to consider the Christian virtue of forbearance or long-suffering. It is much more than patience. The man who is ready to suffer long is, in a special way, slow — he is, for example, slow to anger. The virtue of long-suffering is revealed again and again in the Old Testament. In Exodus, for instance, we read that God is "merciful and gracious, slow to anger and abounding in steadfast love and faithfulness" (Exod. 34. 6).

If God is long-suffering, he suffers insults and offences, but does not punish them. If man is long-suffering, he is slow to anger as God is. Just as God himself, in his forbearance, gives us enough time to find him, so too must we give one another this same time. If this long-suffering, this virtue that is greater and slower than patience, is allowed to grow in us, it will become clear that God, whose nature cannot be explained in purely human terms, has power over our hearts. We should aim therefore to be long-suffering, not only when we feel the urge and not just from time to time, but constantly. We should practise it when we are tired, even exhausted, and when we are feeling faded and weak.

REPENTANCE

Ultimately, however, we can only be fully set free from the guilt of our past in and by love. We must above all be conscious of the words of redemption, which tell us, quite simply: I love you in spite of, and in everything that clings to you from the past. What can guilty man say in answer to this love? Perhaps the only words that he can speak are those in which his redemption is to be found: Lord, I am not worthy of your love.

It is within the framework of this statement and our response to it that our redemption will be brought about, since this is how man, in his guilt, will become aware that the ultimate and most profound element in his being is removed from the sphere of evil. In the light of this knowledge, he will be able to understand what is really evil in his past. His past, especially the evil part of it, will not cease to exist. On the contrary, it will continue to make itself felt in his being as a man. In the sphere of his being as a person, in which he is most completely himself, however, everything is radically changed. Even the significance of what remains of his evil past is transformed. Man is able, from this point onwards, to live his life as it has become on the basis of quite different promises. What is it that in fact takes place in repentance? It is that man turns towards God, consciously or even unconsciously, without knowing explicitly anything about God himself.

A short digression is necessary at this point, if we are to understand why it is that, in our Christian lives, what is great always takes place in what is small, and success in near failure. Let us consider some New Testament texts in which Christ defines the dynamism of the kingdom of God in clear, vivid terms. Many of these parables of the kingdom can be found in the thirteenth chapter of Matthew's gospel, for example: "The kingdom of heaven is like a grain of mustard seed which a man took and sowed in his field; it is the smallest of all seeds, but when it has grown it is the greatest of shrubs and becomes a tree" (Matt. 13. 31-32); "The kingdom of heaven is like a treasure hidden in a field, which a man found and covered up; then in his joy he goes and sells all that he has and buys that field" (Matt. 13.44). Others are found elsewhere in other gospels. In Mark for instance, we read: "The kingdom of God is as if a man should scatter seed upon the ground, and should sleep and rise night and day, and the seed should sprout and grow, he knows not how. The earth produces it of itself, first the blade, then the ear, then the full grain in the ear" (Mark 4. 26-28).

It is obvious from these examples what kind of life Christ wanted to create in us and what kind of norm he wanted to suggest to us as a means of judging the events that take place in the world and in ourselves. On the basis of our faith, then, and the parables of the kingdom, we ought to recognize that even an insignificant, almost hidden movement of the heart such as repentance possesses enough power to shape or transform history and we ought perhaps also to value it more than any other, more striking powers that are present in the world.

Nothing new is totally strange to the Christian. He is not bound to any of the "former things" or to any of the "things of old". In other words, he is not irrevocably committed to any existing form of society or any historically conditioned way of thinking or acting. Christianity is an essentially new and creative attitude which is fundamentally open to all that is good and embraces the whole of life. As Christians we are constantly born anew, but this new birth cannot take place within us until the power of the "things of old" has been broken. This power, moreover, will never be broken as long as it is present in us in the form of guilt. We must therefore rid ourselves of all guilt and above all cease to torment ourselves.

"Behold, I am doing a new thing", God tells us. It may not

yet have struck us forcibly enough that God's dealings with man began with an extremely old man, Abraham, and his old wife, Sarah, both of whom laughed aloud at the thought that a son would be born to them. In the same way, we may not yet have noticed that hardly a single child figures in the whole of the Old Testament, which tells almost exclusively of wise and experienced men. Yet all god's ways in the "Old" Testament lead to a child who was laid in a manger, to a child who as a young man — for Jesus never became old — loved children and gave them to us as an example, to our Lord Jesus Christ, who died as a young man.

The first revelation made in the "New" Testament, then, was that God could be young. Christian perfection is ultimately to be found in our readiness to listen to the voice of God speaking in the events of our own lives and in our refusal to allow that voice to be silenced by the guiltiness of a past which has become fossilized in us. Christ has made rivers of grace flow through the desert of our world. He spoke too of his friendship in the image of new wine that should not be put in old bottles. Indeed, with Christ something so powerful and dynamic has entered our lives that all previous moulds have burst and are still bursting.

"Create in me a clean heart, O God, and put a new spirit within me", the psalmist sings (Ps 51.10) and these words tell us a great deal about repentance and prayer. This longing for a pure heart strikes us nowadays as strange and outdated. It certainly cannot mean a heart that is able to confront the powers of our modern world. All men are looking, on the other hand, for a new spirit, for they are anxious to set about the task of creating a fundamentally new society and of doing this in a new spirit. So that part of the psalmist's petition arouses an echo today in our minds. But a pure heart — what is that, we ask? The deep confusion of the age in which we live is, however, in my opinion, expressed in this dilemma that we experience when we consider the psalmist's longing for a pure heart and a new spirit.

If we, as Christians, have anything at all to offer the world, it is a pure heart. A new spirit is created, one might almost say, automatically from a pure heart. What, then is this pure heart that is mentioned in the psalm? It is not simply by chance that the heart has come to be regarded as the supreme symbol of the central reality of man. Man's heart represents the interconnection between his body and soul and between his inner attitude and his outward actions. The pure heart of the psalm points therefore to the truthfulness of our life as man, to the sincerity of our existence in this world, to the honesty of our prayer to God and to whether our attitude towards ourselves, God and our fellow-men is pure. We can have a pure heart so long as we let ourselves be tested and examined by God. Repentance is therefore clearly not something that can be undertaken by those who are weak.

Seen in this light, repentance is an attitude brought about by a purity of heart, which cannot be cramped by the narrowness or pettiness existing in our own lives and which, on the contrary, "puts a new spirit within us". We ought therefore to ask Christ again and again to give us a pure heart, an attitude which is fundamentally noble and which looks to the future, so that we shall be able, in a new spirit, to fashion the future and create a new society. It is only if we have a pure heart that we shall be able to build up a new world. A pure heart and a new spirit belong indissolubly together.

Last things

In this chapter I shall talk about the Christian mysteries that are usually known by the title of "the last things".

SIN OF LIFE

Before we can speak about heaven in human terms, we must first consider a number of relevant questions. The first has to do with sin as the obstacle which prevents us from entering heaven. My own point of view is that our sin does not consist of our many individual acts of rebellion. It is not of "sins" that we have to speak here, but rather of man's almost imperceptible slipping into an unhappy state of wrongness. I call this process the "sin of life". In it, we gradually become thick-skinned, insensitive and hard.

Each step leading us deeper into this state of wrongness enables us to tell ourselves with greater outward conviction that our Christian duty impels us to act in this way. But that process at the same time brings us nearer to a situation in which we are so inwardly dissatisfied with ourselves that we are no longer capable of looking forward to any greater and deeper fulfilment.

The most important aspect of this sin of life, however, is that it is not conspicuous or dramatic. It is very easy for anyone to admit that he is a great sinner. There are levels of existence, however, at which it is difficult for us to recognize ourselves and come to a decision about ourselves, and periods of existential weakness at which it is similarly difficult to translate such decisions into action. Although, in such cases, the individual expressions of our inner being can only be classified, according to the earlier structures of moral theology, under the heading of "venial" sins, our whole life may be no more than a lie.

Like many others, I have tried several times to work out a theory of man's death which will make it quite clear that the way to heaven is open to all men. Reduced to its basic essentials, this hypothesis points to the fact that death makes it possible for a man to act for the first time fully as a person, and that it is the privileged place where he is able, in the depths of his being, to become fully conscious, to achieve complete freedom, to encounter Christ and to decide about his eternal destiny.

In the light of this hypothesis, it is clear that the salvation brought to us by Christ is really open to us all. It is a universal salvation in which every person, without a single exception, can, in complete possession of all his powers, in complete clarity and freedom, make a decision concerning Christ. We should therefore be able to use this hypothesis to reflect in a new way about the important theological questions of our membership of the Church, the meaning of the sacraments, the universal nature of redemption and our own personal relationship with Christ.

PURGATORY

An understanding of death as our breakthrough to God is an understanding of the event we call purgatory. When we die, all the wrongness that we have accumulated within us collapses and we are exposed to what we really are, to what is eternal in our existence. Our wealth and belongings, our power and strength and all our success vanish. At death, the while of our being is handed over to what at that moment still remains to us — our longing, our cry for help and forgiveness.

At the moment of death, we know that all that remains of us is what we have already given up. Only our selflessness is left. Sometimes it is the most insignificant experiences in our lives which become significant when we are dying — the hours spent with a suffering friend, the incomprehensible mystery of pain and sorrow, the occasions when we gave ourselves totally in friendship and love, our sharing in the humanity of our fellow men.

Purgatory can be defined as a momentary process of becoming truly ourselves in the deep abyss of death. By encountering ourselves in complete openness and honesty, and in encountering ourselves, we behold Christ himself. This meeting with Christ may be called, quite simply, the judgment.

JUDGMENT

This judgment is the revelation of the dimension of Christ himself in our being. Matthew tells us that the righteous — and that surely also applies to the unrighteous — asked Christ: "Lord, when did we see thee hungry and feed thee or thirsty and give thee to drink" (Matt. 25. 37 ff). When, we may ask, did we do all these things to "one of the least of the brethren"? We have, I think, almost always done the greatest things without really taking account of them. Our encounter with Christ takes place in the hidden part of our lives.

The ultimate depth of everything that we experience and hope and long for in friendship and love and that we do in selfless help of others is Christ himself. In the judgment that follows death, man is confronted with his own eternal being and with the discovery that all the good that he has done and intended is a dimension of Christ, that his impulses are in reality God's impulses. Nothing else counts at that moment, and nothing prevents man from entering a state of complete joy. In the last judgment, all things are put right. How simple things are ultimately if judgment is seen as a message of joy. Yet many people have been prevented from entering into the promise of the good news by the mere word "judgment".

HELL

It is important to understand that hell is not something that happens to us or that God imposes on us later because of our misdeeds. It is neither great nor external. It is simply man identifying himself entirely with what he has become and with what he can accomplish and obtain by force on his own. It is the mode of existence of a man who is completely satisfied with and in himself for eternity. It is the everlasting state of a man who has no more and desires no more than himself alone.

Above all, hell is not an external threat, because hell cannot be a "place". There is an attitude of mind and heart, and everything must live in heaven because God has created the world in the direction of heaven. That heaven is the world made translucent by and for God, and we experience it in the light of our inner disposition. If we have become poor, we shall be able to grasp its beauty; but if we have remained rich, we shall have to remain satisfied with our own wealth. If, on the other hand, we can receive more and give ourselves more and more in love, we shall live in eternal happiness, the happiness of being able to love for ever. We shall be in heaven. If we lack the courage to love, we shall not be able to sustain heaven. The only word that has any eternal validity is love.

RESURRECTION

Resurrection is the complete fulfilment of life. Man's bodily existence becomes personal. Seeing becomes knowing, contact becomes recognition and hearing becomes understanding. We can sense what it is to be really man in this way in the figure of the risen Christ, who has overcome all the limitations of purely external life. Christ's resurrection was above all not just a return – it was a complete transformation of his being. According to my hypothesis, we may say that man decides his own eternity and immortality in the decision that he takes at death. The consequence of this is – and once again I must ask the reader not to take offence at what I say, since it is completely orthodox – that we should not cling stubbornly to the idea that the human soul is naturally immortal. A more positive thought is that, in this decision, man throws himself into the personal "You" of God, in other words, into what is eternal and immortal, so that his immortality becomes much more than mere "immortality". It becomes an entirely personal event in which man is a unity of body and soul. This immortality is at the same time resurrection. Seen in this way, there is no difference between immortality and resurrection.

Resurrection takes place at death

Death has often been regarded by Christians as the separation of the soul from the body, but, in the light of what has just been said, this view does not go far enough and is even erroneous. Man does not, after all, consist of two things. He is one, and matter and spirit are indissolubly united in his being. From these two united elements comes a third that is neither the one nor the other. The human soul enters matter with an inner necessity that forms an essential part of its nature and it is this that makes it "soul". Man's body is an essential act of the soul, which is not a thing, but an essential relationship with matter. Man is as I have said, one body-soul, and, to put it bluntly but correctly, nothing is left of man without his body. This is why the transition that takes place at the moment of death, the definitive decision that man makes then, must be regarded as the moment of resurrection. If that is true, then the consequence is that:

Resurrection must be universal

The universe is concentrated within us and we are part of the universe. We are entirely children of this earth. It is not simply the space in which we are able to develop as independent beings. It also belongs totally to our constitution, just as our body and soul together belong to our being. If immortality takes place with our soul, it must be resurrection. If resurrection occurs with our body, it must also be transfiguration of the whole universe. This means that:

Christ is still coming

Christ will not reach his full cosmic age until all of us, the whole human race, who constitute the fulness of his being — or, as Paul says, his pleroma — have encountered him in the final unity of creative love. Then the longing of all men and of the whole world will be fulfilled and God will be "all in all".

HEAVEN

What do we gain by extending our experience of and in the world to include heaven? We achieve a spiritual togetherness with God, an integration into the infinite life of God of everything that lives and grows emotionally and intellectually in the world.

The endless happiness of this heavenly existence is shown in Revelation: "I will be his God and he shall be my son"; "I will grant to him to sit with me on my throne"; the blessed will "shine like the sun". In the gospel of John this union with God is described vividly: "If a man loves me, he will keep my word, and my Father will love him, and we will come to him and make our home with him" (John 14. 23) and in Luke's gospel as a banquet: "You may eat and drink at my table in my kingdom" (Luke 22. 30). This state of final, endless blessedness is described in the New Testament in images of happiness, purity, clarity and life.

Let us try to penetrate into the mystery in Christ's prayer at the Last Supper: "O righteous Father, the world has not known thee, but I have known thee; and these know that thou hast sent me. I made known to them thy name, and I will make it known, that the love with which thou hast loved me (in other words, the Holy Spirit) may be in them, and I in them" (John 17. 25–26).

This love of Christ in us will, in heaven, become eternal being. We hardly dare to say what this will mean in terms of deep, glowing intensity of existence. Whether we are immortal by nature and what form the world will take when it rises again to new being — this is perhaps important, but it is not, in the last resort, of supreme importance. What is supremely important is that we love God and that God loves us with a love that is infinite and all-embracing. It is this love that becomes ours, our very being for eternity.

With the resurrection of Christ, the end of time began. If we are to remain faithful to our call to love God, we have to try to live here and now in the light of heaven. It is our destiny as Christians and our mission to live heaven now.

Although various words and phrases are used in the Bible — the kingdom of heaven, the land of the living, consolation, infinite mercy, fellowship with God and so on — the same promise is made by the God who became man. It is the promise of life itself. The Bible also shows us the way to that life with God — abandonment of ourselves, gentleness, peace-making and above all a hunger and thirst for justice. All these are, after all, qualities of love and it is in this love that man will receive by giving himself.

This outline of the nature of heaven is, of necessity, rather fragmentary, but it leads us directly to an urgent question — how can heaven be proclaimed nowadays to our fellow men?

MODERN MAN

The twentieth century is marked by technology and science, and modern man has been profoundly influenced in every way by the advances made in this sphere. There can also be no doubt that his attitude towards the world will continue to be changed radically in the future because of these advances. There is little to be gained from lamenting this fact or from being glad about it. We have simply to accept it as a datum and then try to pinpoint those aspects of modern technological man especially attuned to the preaching of the Christian message and of heaven. In his work of redemption here and now, God clearly has modern technological man in mind and wants him to be able to enter heaven.

Sense of purpose

The first aspect of modern man which provides a point of contact with the Christian message is his deep sense of purpose, his consciousness of the tasks that confront him. He is always looking towards an end, and is tenacious, persistent, conscientious and disciplined in his determination to achieve it. Everything that he does is planned and all his actions are dictated by his attitude towards his work.

Objectivity

Modern man's sense of purpose is closely connected with another fundamental characteristic — his objectivity. He is acutely aware of the impulse that comes to him from the object and listens attentively to the objective truth. His attitude is one of intense concentration on the things of this world, and these things in turn fashion him. He is able to contemplate and assess the value of the object only by firmly excluding his subjective feelings. There is, moreover, no room in this attitude for approximations. In a word, twentieth-century man is able only to deal with objective data. Otherwise his work is in danger of being destroyed.

Self-giving

In his resolute objectivity, modern man tends to give himself freely. In his attempt to get away from subjectivity, he has, as it were, to leave himself out of account. The decisive element is his work. In his determination to complete it, he is never lenient with himself. All his knowledge, he insists, must come from the object itself. He excludes all arbitrary factors and overcomes all desire to obtain power.

Sobriety

All these aspects of contemporary man's attitude culminate in one all-important characteristic: his sobriety. The present generation is less trusting and more sceptical than previous generations. Modern man is not prepared to take risks with what he has so laboriously and objectively built up. He is aware of the firm foundation to society laid by his technological skill, knowledge and discipline. Yet he is conscious of the presence, in almost every other sphere of his activity today — in philosophy, the arts and social studies, politics and religion — of heated discussion and conflicting views. Modern technological man is convinced that the human community of the future will be saved from the chaos that threatens it and built up on the basis of an objective vision, a concentration on what is essential, and strict self-discipline.

Organization

An important aspect of a modern man closely linked to that sobriety is an attitude based on objective discipline. He accepts this need to become an integral part of a working plan. His work is of paramount importance and makes enormous demands on him, especially in organization and planning. But his attitude, can never be one of subordination to work or of taking orders from others. It is not possible, in a modern, technically-orientated and highly-organized business or industry, to issue orders and expect them to be obeyed unquestioningly. There are no workers in industry today who just obey orders. Everyone is directed, on equal terms, by an objective discipline which is inherent in the task itself. The more complicated that task is, the more closely the individuals working in the industry have to collaborate in groups and communities. Each individual has to work with extreme precision within his own specialization, and the final product is the result of the joint effort of all individuals.

Raw material

The last and perhaps the most important aspect of modern man to which all the others seem to point is his attitude to the world. His vision includes the whole world, not only in the sense of a planetary society, but in that of a cosmic affinity. He does not recognize any part of the world as closed to him. The infinite starry spaces of the universe, the sub-atomic structure of matter, and the biological and psychological nature of man are all included within his plans. He even hopes to use his power to transform the world so that man himself is an object of planning. It is not wrong to say that modern man regards both the world as it is and himself as the "raw material" for the creation of a new world and a new man in accordance with his own plans.

It is precisely this twentieth-century man, fashioned by science and technology, whom Christ came to redeem. It is God's intention that this man should be able to enter heaven. What are his positive aspects?

GREATNESS OF MAN

The greatness of the world has been revealed to modern man, who is dedicated to it, and "listens" to it. His silence is an expression of concentrated power. Everything petty and narrow seems unacceptable. We have to ask how long contemporary man will be able to endure the unworthy, narrow-minded, philistine image of God which he has so often been given. The experience of carrying out his great task gives man a deep confidence. He sees himself as serving the future and fashioning a new world. He is dominated by the ethical idea of selfless service. He does not work for himself, but for others. The product of his work will be used by other people.

A final positive characteristic of contemporary man is that he looks towards and lives for the future. However threatening the world may seem, he feels sure that he will be able to control it. So long as he faithfully adheres to the laws of naure and carries out his work carefully and exactly, success, he believes, is certain. Clearly, his attitude towards the world is marked by a new kind of recollectedness — the serene firmness of a man who is exposed to the dangerous forces of nature, but who is confident tht he will be able to master them. He is, however, convinced that the world is good and that man will be safe so long as he obeys the laws that underlie the world and nature and fashion the future in accordance with them. This conviction may perhaps mark the point at which modern man penetrates furthest into the metaphysical religious sphere of understanding.

A great deal is, of course, left out of this description of the positive aspects of contemporary man's attitude towards the world. It does not, for instance, include any suggestion of anideal portrait of modern man, and some of the characteristics mentioned may strike us as strange and even as impoverished. Nevertheless, a Christian ought to see in this new pattern of human life and attitude towards the world and people a sign of God's grace which is entirely appropriate to our age.

The opening address made by Pope John XXIII at the Second Vatican Council was an affirmation of this new open attitude of twentieth-century man: "In the daily exercise of our pastoral office, we sometimes have to listen, much to our regret, to voices of people, who, though burning with zeal, are not endowed with too much sense of discretion or measure. In these modern times they can see nothing but prevarication and ruin. They say that our era, in comparison with past eras, is getting worse and they behave as though they had learned nothing from history, which is, nonetheless, the teacher of life. . . . We feel that we must disagree with those prophets of gloom, who are always forecasting disaster. . . . In the present order of things, divine providence is leading us to a new order of human relations which, by men's own efforts and even beyond their very expectations are directed towards the fulfilment of God's superior and inscrutable designs".

I feel that we ought to speak in this way to modern man about heaven and at the same time make use of the positive characteristics mentioned above — his silence, his confidence and his recollectedness. All these characteristics are clearly signs of his greatness. They are also qualities which enable us to claim, less by our words than by the witness we bear, that modern man is moving towards a future which will never be superseded and is absolute. At the same time contemporary man has other characteristics, or "points of support", which enable us to speak to him even more convincingly about heaven.

PROCLAMATION OF HEAVEN

The first point of support is that every man is given the grace to imitate Christ. Every man carries his cross insofar as he is a man. A Christian is a man who takes up the cross of his own free will, saying perhaps: this is right for me; I must take up my misery because Christ, my Lord, did the same. — That attitude enables the kingdom of Christ to come about in the world and from that kingdom heaven will grow. Authentic life can only arise when man accepts a demand, and that demand is almost always the cross.

I believe that modern man understands this very well. All of us fail and must inevitably fail in some aspect of our lives. Christians, however, are able and have to fail because of love. The courage to ask Christ to be allowed to do that to the point where we are humbled as he was humbled or at least to want to be able to ask him for this attitude is fundamentally the courage to be a Christian. Claiming something greater is the only way to greatness.

But following Christ in that way is not something

exceptional or extraordinary. We all encounter the cross at different times and usually in small ways. A Christian is a person who, consciously or unconsciously, says Yes to imitating Christ by carrying the cross. The road to heaven is by way of the cross. I think that contemporary man is fully aware of this and would even agree openly with it. And the cross for the most part consists simply of adapting oneself to whatever life presents and persevering on the course that one has to follow.

A second point of support for our proclamation of the message of heaven is this. We can learn from Mary the lesson of acceptance. Christ was taken down from the cross and, according to tradition, Mary received him in her lap. What did she think about, seeing her son there? No doubt she looked back at her own life. Like all people in this world, she led a life which was a restless process of becoming and passing away, filled with sorrow and tears on the one hand and moments of happiness on the other, but for the most part consisting of very ordinary experiences, so that one hour followed the other, seemingly empty and often dull.

Now, however, holding the dead Christ, all this must have seemed somehow insignificant to her and she could only have been aware of the fact that the world had been made open to God. At the end, she expected one final gift and, without denying or rejecting any moment of her earthly life, she entered heaven and everlasting life. I think that modern man, who is happy to give his life totally in the service of others, can quite easily understand this example and, like Mary, simply accept his own very ordinary life as a gift from God and see in it the promise of eternal life and heaven. (Of course, non-Christians might not so easily understand the precise reference to Mary herself).

The third point of support that I should like to discuss

briefly is joy. Heaven is made open to us in the Easter event. Since Easter, the attitude which underlies all the other attitudes of the Christian believer and which dominates his entire existence is a fundamental orientation towards joy. His whole experience of life, including that of suffering and death, is inevitably contained within this basic orientation. Where that joy exists, perhaps only implicitly or unconsciously, our Lord Jesus Christ is present and, with him, his definitive promise of heaven.

In that sense every man experiences heaven in his inmost being, whether he is a baptized Christian or not. But it is the task of a conscious Christian to live on earth in the light of heaven and therefore to radiate joy in the world. A Christian bears witness to his faith in the world by experiencing heaven as the most real of all realities and by enabling his fellow men to believe in that reality. In doing that, we shall not only enter heaven ourselves, but make it possible for our friends to share our faith in it now and enter it themselves.

All the truths that I have discussed in this chapter can be interpreted more negatively. It may be that I have overlooked the sadder aspects of my subject. But every one of us has his own way of interpreting the truth, and mine is positive. I have tried to reconcile opposites. But I would ask whether "wisdom" is merely a knowledge of the darker side of man's existence. Is Christian "philosophy" (the love of wisdom) exclusively sad?

The Eucharist

The sacrament of the Eucharist, Holy Communion, the Mass, or the Lord's Supper, is a highly-concentrated reality, embracing the whole of Christian life in its many aspects. It has universally human and cosmic dimensions. It embodies all the essential elements of the other sacraments. It is the pre-eminent place where we are able to encounter God.

If the Eucharist is of such central importance in the life of a Christian community, it cannot be easy to do justice to it in a short article. There is only one way of speaking meaningfully about the Eucharist. That is to consider individual aspects of the sacrament in turn, at the same time trying to maintain a view of the whole.

SACRED BANQUET

Banquet

The first and absolutely fundamental aspect of the Eucharist is that it is essentially a meal. What we are primarily celebrating in the Eucharist is man's togetherness with other men.

It is a common opinion nowadays that this human community that we celebrate in the Eucharist is the product of an evolutionary process that has lasted for thousands of millions of years and the summit of an immense and universal effort. That process is still moving towards even higher stages of development. At a very high level of evolution is the ability of man to love and to be together in love and friendship with his fellow men. At this stage, man is really able — and not simply figuratively able — to become one with his fellows. This is indeed the great mystery of the human spirit — that it can become one.

According to Christian teaching, love is universal, embracing the whole of mankind. All men are called to love and the whole universe is raised to an entirely new state. With the coming of Christianity the evolution of the cosmos is brought to a final and unsurpassable climax at which the whole human community is united. This culminating point of the evolutionary process is reached in all-embracing love as the expression of man's ultimate togetherness. Wherever men are gathered together in the celebration of the Eucharist, an event of universal significance takes place. The whole evolution of the cosmos has from the beginning been directed towards that end. In the celebration of the Eucharist, the universe enters a new stage of its development and we who are present absorb into our existence the forces of this evolution and are thus empowered to lead the universe towards its ultimate fulfilment. The Eucharist is the culmination of the beauty, effort, suffering and longing of the world.

In the Eucharist, we celebrate this universal event in the form of a banquet. We should, however, always bear in mind that a banquet or festive meal is not simply a culinary event. It is above all a spiritual and culinary event at the same time, where people eat and drink together and talk in a human and brotherly way during the meal. Sometimes, during the banquet, the conversation really gets going and the ultimate questions of man's existence are discussed. This situation is described in Plato's Symposium. In the banquet of the Eucharist, our position in the universe becomes clear to us. We recognize ourselves as integral parts of the natural world and as communicating with it by eating and drinking. At the same time, however, we are aware that we are raised far above the world and are in communion with God. The essential meaning of the term "banquet" can be reduced to this — that we contain the world within ourselves and yet go beyond it.

Sacred

What is sacred or holy is what is in contact with God and shares in God. The evolution of the universe is sacred or holy because, from the beginning, there has always been a conscious tendency, according to God's plan, for creation to ascend in man to the spiritual sphere and, through this conscious decision to choose God, to come more and more closely in contact with God and to share in God. We men are called by God's love to contain the movement of the universe towards holiness within us and are therefore the culminating point of the development of the universe at which holiness is achieved. It is only in and through us that the universe can reach holiness. What happens in our banquet, then, is that our togetherness on the one hand and the evolution of the universe on the other are brought together, summed up and celebrated. This process arouses in us a profound desire to extend evolution, so that we will eventually reach a total unity of being with God. Inspired by this evolutionary urge, we long, in other words, to achieve what is, to all appearances, impossible. How can that be done?

Throughout his long history, man has always been seeking to become one with God. He has constantly longed to make something sacred and this aspiration has long been known as *sacrificium,* literally "making sacred", although this original meaning is heavily disguised in our words "sacrifice" or "offering". What man has always wanted to do, in offering sacrifice, is to carry out an action that is sufficiently powerful to penetrate as far as God himself. For thousands of years, man has offered sacrifice in his almost desperate attempts to break through to God and many of these efforts have taken forms which often strike us now as absurd or frightening. Under the almost imperceptible influence of the Holy Spirit, however, a certain basic structure that is common to most forms of sacrifice has emerged.

If he is to come into contact with God and his absolute holiness, man has to set aside everything in him that is unworthy and unclean. He must be converted. Secondly, he has to bring together all that is best in his existence and offer it to God. To do this, he needs a symbolic gift, an earthly reality which he can separate from all other objects in the world and give to God. At the same time, he identifies himself with this gift so that he is that offering. In the third place, a transformation has to take place. This is the moment when God intervenes in the process by accepting man's gift and indeed by accepting man himself in and through the sacrificial gift.

The transformation takes place in this acceptance of man by God — what is earthly is transformed into what is divine. The fourth essential element in the sacrificial structure is communion. After having accepted the offering and having changed it into himself, making it divine, God gives the gift back to man. This completes the circle of the sacrifice. Man has entered, in his sacrifice, into a unity of being with God: in other words, he is in communion with him. What is more, he (and with and through him the whole universe) is made holy through this sacrifice or "making sacred".

This basic sacrificial structure has been transformed by the action of Christ who has, in his life, death and resurrection, brought everything that is authentically and truly human to completion. He might have been able to find an entirely new and different way to God, but he did not. Instead, he took the whole of man's experience and completed it, giving it a deeper meaning. Since he has come, all our efforts to become united with God through sacrifice have been brought to fulfilment. The whole sacrificial process is clearly recognizable in Christ's transformation and fulfilment of it in the celebration of the Eucharist. What is more, since Christ's coming, man (and through him the whole universe) is no longer united in his sacrifice with an unknown and undefined God. He is united with the risen Christ.

CHRIST IS RECEIVED

Let us now see how these four essential aspects of the sacri-fice are expressed so that they point to Christ.

Conversion

At the very beginning of the Eucharist, the priest or minister usually calls upon the people to ask for God's forgiveness, and the whole community prays for God's mercy. There are many other occasions when the priest expresses this need for forgiveness and conversion. Before reading the gospel, he prays that the Lord may be in people's hearts and on their lips. He and the people prepare for the sacred meal by saying together the Lord's Prayer: "Forgive us our trespasses . . . and lead us not into temptation, but deliver us from evil".

In eucharistic prayers, man as it were tries to reach the uppermost point of holiness in Jesus Christ, throwing aside everything that might hold him back in this movement upwards towards heaven. At the same time, he also gathers together everything from the movement of the universe that has been created from the beginning in Christ and has ever longed to find fulfilment as the body of Christ. In this longing experienced by Christians for purity, we see the longing of creation of which Paul speaks in the eighth chapter of his letter to the Romans. The whole of creation is redeemed by our gathering in ourselves all that is best and most pure in the universe and then turning in humility towards Christ our Lord, so that, in us, the world can be brought to the one who has redeemed and completed it.

Offering

This whole movement is brought to a climax in the offering, when we take bread and wine as symbols for ourselves and the world that has produced us, nourished us and kept us in being and offer them to the Lord. God is asked to accept these gifts for his praise and for the salvation of the whole world and to accept us and make us a sacrifice that is pleasing to him. In the words of the offertory prayer of the Roman rite, "May we have fellowship in the divinity of him (Christ), who deigned to share our humanity". We can look confidently forward to being incorporated into the risen and transfigured body of the Lord. We can be sure that the wall of our corruptible nature will be broken down and that we shall be carried towards eternal fulfilment.

Transformation

It is at this point that the mystery which comprises the whole of our faith and which we therefore describe as the "mystery of faith" is enacted. Christ fills the sacrificial gifts in such a way with his powerful, all-penetrating presence that they even lose their proper substance and become him. The bread and wine that we offer are raised up and drawn into the very life of God. They are taken up into heaven, in other words, they filled to the very brim of their being by Christ.

These offerings are ourselves and, through us, the whole world. This is a hidden or mysterious reality, since it is concealed by the visible forms of bread and wine, but it is still a reality and indeed the most real of all realities. The altar on earth and the altar in heaven, that is, heaven and earth, are now united. Earth has been transformed into heaven. It has become the body of the risen Christ.

Communion

During the offering in the Eucharist, earth reaches upwards towards heaven. At the time of communion, it is heaven that inclines itself to earth. Christ gives himself to man and through man to the whole world. It is only at this moment that the circle of the eucharistic sacrifice is closed – at the moment of communion, when Christ becomes entirely ours in our innermost being. It is not wrong to say that, in communion, he becomes mine with all his living and holy existence. He becomes the source and principle of my life and I receive his being, body and soul, in myself and begin to exist entirely from him. Christ – his whole life as he is, with all his thoughts, desires, feelings and sensations – becomes the bread of our lives. We in turn penetrate into his being, into the Christ whose fulness, we are told by Paul in his letter to the Ephesians, "fills all in all".

We, however, all receive the same Lord in communion and make him part of our innermost being together. That means that we become one with each other: a single risen body. At the same time, we are united in communion with everything that the Lord fills with his presence. What takes place at the moment of communion is what Paul described as the most profound mystery of the shared life of the Christian community. As Christians, we are integrated in communion into the risen body of Christ and through communion we grow together as a community into one single being. The whole Eucharist is directed towards that meal shared with each other. Its end is communion.

Received

The Eucharist is to be "received". It is much more than simply the consecration of bread for adoration. In it, Christ becomes our bread of life. There can be no doubt that our communion is an integral part of the sacrifice and that it should be an act of personal communication with God. As Hugh of Saint Victor said, "Christ should not rest in your stomach, but in your spirit". In communion, our personal union with Christ ought to be made stronger and our personal relationship with him nourished, intensified and preserved. Indeed, that personal relationship with Christ is the beginning and the end of our life as Christians; it is towards that essential relationship that the whole sacrament is directed.

Frequent communion comes very close to the furthest limit of its meaning when man, in the situation in which he finds himself in the world, is both inwardly and outwardly no longer capable, in all good will, of preparing himself for and responding to a more frequent reception of the sacrament. The grace which comes to man from receiving the Eucharist is a grace leading to a deeper personal communication with Christ. Because of this the essential meaning of the sacrament ceases for the mature Christian at the point where he reaches the furthest possible limit at which he is capable of receiving the Eucharist with an intense response. If that is true, the opposite is also true. If this personal communication between the believer and the risen Christ is increased by a frequent reception of the sacrament, then that man should clearly receive the Eucharist more frequently, until the limit is reached. That inner possibility of growth should be the governing factor, and the observation and guidance of it is a task which may be shared between the Christian himself in a process of cautious self-criticism and a sensitive and intelligent spiritual director.

I conclude this section with a pertinent passage from the writings of Augustine: "If one man says that the Lord's Supper should be received every day and another says the opposite, then every man should do what he thinks he ought to do in piety according to his faith. Zacchaeus and the centurion were not at cross-purposes with each other when the first received the Lord joyfully in his house and the second said: I am not worthy that you should come under my roof. Both gave honour to the Redeemer, but not in the same way".

HIS PASSION IS CELEBRATED

Commemoration

The Eucharist is not an isolated event. It is a mystery which goes back far into the past history of man's salvation; it is above all a commemorative celebration. After the departure of their Lord, the first Christians were in the habit of meeting together as a community. At these meetings, the disciples of the Lord who were still alive narrated his words and deeds. They called to mind the unforgettable hours that they had spent with him while he was still among them. Their offering of the Eucharist was deeply embedded in this situation of being together and remembering and thinking about the Lord. That loving recollection of Christ was not, however, simply a happy dwelling on the past. Remembering Christ made him really present for the early Christians, just as remembering him makes him present for us today.

This assertion can be justified theologically without difficulty. As a man who was entirely subject, like all men, to the normal course of human history, Christ embodied an anticipation of the future. Because it existed in a personal unity with the Logos, Christ's human soul, as an act of supreme knowledge, beheld the Father. Within this beholding of the Father, there was, in Christ's soul, which was both human and divine, a knowledge of salvation that was so powerful and all-embracing that time and space receded from it and the whole of human history became present. From that knowledge, which was in fact not only a knowledge, but also included feeling, loving, willing and being together, Christ came close to us men in love, received our life into his own and bore it in his heart. Although we were not alive at that time, we were nonetheless present in Christ. Bringing about this presence in Christ is called celebrating the Eucharist. Christ's life is made present for us because our lives were already present in Christ.

That act of remembering, however, goes even further back into the past and we call to mind the whole of the history of our salvation from Old Testament times until the coming of Christ. All this great movement that took place under God's guidance is made present in the eucharistic prayer, in which we recall the "gifts of God's servant Abel, the sacrifice of Abraham, our father in faith, and the bread and wine offered by God's priest Melchisedech". In the Eucharist, then, the great historical movement of the universe in the past towards salvation becomes present here and now. All that salvation-history flows together in Christ who, Paul tells us in his letter to the Christians of Colossus, is "the first-born of all creation, for in him all things were created . . . all things were created through him and in him" (Col. 1. 15—16) and in whom, as the Apostle says in his letter to the Ephesians, "all things are united, things in heaven and things on earth" (Eph. 1. 10). This making present of the entire history of man's salvation is, however, directed above all towards the central event in the life of Christ, his suffering.

Passion

This word is used as a part standing for the whole. The greater reality is composed of four individual aspects: death, descent, resurrection and ascension. This fourfold unity, this single act with four aspects, is celebrated in the Eucharist as the central event of our redemption. Immediately after the consecration of the bread and wine, the priest prays: "Father, we celebrate the memory of Christ, your Son. We, your people and your ministers, recall his passion, his resurrection from the dead, and his ascension into glory". If we are to believe the testimony of Paul, it was in this act that Christ, as a man and not simply as the second person of the divine Trinity, became "the head over all things" (Eph. 1. 22) and the one who brings the universe to completion.

Christ broke through the limitations of our tangible reality in his death and, in his descent "into hell", he penetrated into the innermost reality of the world. In his resurrection, his body acquired universal dimensions and a cosmic power and, as a man, he achieved eternal life. Finally, in his ascension, he took the whole world with him towards eternal existence. In these four stages, then, Christ brought about the salvation of the entire universe in a final and definitive cosmic action. It was, as it were, a passage through death, corruptibility and the world into future glory and heaven. According to the author of the letter to the Hebrews, this action was that of Christ as our great high priest. Finally, it is precisely this action that is made present in the Eucharist.

The past history of our salvation, in particular Christ's suffering — that is, his death, descent, resurrection and ascension —
is called to mind in the Eucharist and thereby made present.
Through this action:

THE MIND IS FILLED WITH GRACE

Mind

The Latin word for "mind" is *mens,* and this means much
more than "mind" in English. It points to the mysterious,
hidden and innermost being of man's physical and psychical
existence. What is referred to here is that mysterious sphere
in man which includes both aspects of his existence, his body
and his spirit, and which is rooted in both aspects.

The "mind" is therefore that element in man which is
turned towards God, the aspect of his life which is open to
the divine reality, the part of his existence which flows
directly towards the Father. It is that hidden reality which
Paul had in mind when he wrote to the Colossians: "Your
life is hid with Christ in God. When Christ who is our life
appears, then you also will appear with him in glory" (Col. 3.
4). It is precisely this hiding ourselves in Christ that takes
place in the Eucharist — we transfer our whole life, soul and
body, into Christ who is present everywhere, but hidden.
This growing together with Christ, which, though not yet
revealed, is nonetheless real, is what constitutes the particular
grace of the Eucharist.

Grace

For a long time — above all when I was studying theology as
a young man — I was puzzled by the concept of grace. It was
only when I began to take God's incarnation really seriously
and therefore came to understand that, as men, we have the
right to speak of the divine reality in human terms that I

really had a clear insight into the meaning of grace. Then I was able to say with conviction: Grace is in the last resort simply God's friendship. Because of that friendship, we men live in a state of reciprocity with God. If it were not for this reciprocity of our being and God's, we would cease to be human and God would cease to be divine.

The deep mystery of friendship is to be found in the fact that it welds together two beings that are otherwise separate and at the same time confers on each of them full independent being. That grace of God's friendship for us therefore brings us to God himself and enables us to live already, in the hidden depths of our being, in heaven. In this grace, our tale here on earth is already the table of our eternal glory, the altar on earth and the altar in heaven are one. We are already at God's table: in other words, we are already in personal communication with the Trinity. We have entered into God — our life is hidden with Christ in God, as Paul taught.

That means that our own life and that of the world are superseded and that we have finally reached our goal, the Omega point of the universe, as Teilhard de Chardin called it. That is the ultimate dimension: the future dimension of the universe and the completion of the process of our becoming one with Christ. That definitive stage of our development is expressed at the conclusion of Aquinas' antiphon for the feast of the Eucharist:

PLEDGE OF FUTURE GLORY

Future glory

The ultimate completion of history will reveal man in his new state of "glory" and not only man, but the whole universe will, in that final fulfilment, shine forth in glory.

That completion of the universe is simply Jesus Christ himself, the risen Lord. Everything is taken up into Christ, completed in him and revealed in luminous glory. Finally completed, everything becomes Christ's body and the world, mankind and Christ himself form one single bodily unity. Paul called this unity *pleroma*, the fulness of Christ. That state of final perfection — heaven — is already present in a hidden form in the Eucharist. The definitive future of the world has already begun.

This future state, however, is at present hidden in the forms of bread and wine, whereas in heaven it will be definitively revealed. The Eucharist points to this ultimate state of creation. It is the promise of a world in which Christ is no longer hidden and it makes that world already present. In that future world made present in the Eucharist, everything will be drawn into the life of God and be made new. Nothing will perish and everything will be plunged into the reality of Christ, bear and reveal him and exist with him for ever. That is our future glory — an existence as the risen, glorified body of Christ in which we are in eternal communion with God. The Eucharist gives us this eternal glory already, but in a hidden form. That is why Thomas Aquinas uses the word.

Pledge

In the Eucharist, Christ gives himself as a pledge that we shall enter into the glory of heaven.

The really astonishing aspect of the Eucharist is that God places himself in our hands as a hostage, enabling us to compel him, as it were, to bring about the eternal fulfilment of man and the universe and to give us future glory. A piece of bread and a mouthful of wine received in faith: those are the future of the world. It is almost too much to say it aloud. One is afraid of being thought out of one's mind.

And yet the whole of the sixth chapter of the gospel of John is concerned simply with that one fact, that "the bread of God is that which comes down from heaven and gives life to the world" (John 6. 33). At the end of the chapter, we read: "After this many of his disciples drew back and no longer went about with him. Jesus said to the twelve: 'Will you also go away?' Simon Peter answered him, 'Lord, to whom shall we go? You have the words of eternal life; and we have believed, and have come to know, that you are the Holy One of God" (John 6. 66–70).

All that concerns man at the deepest level of his existence: his immortality and the immortality of everything that is dear to him; the immortality of the immortality of the whole of creation. Neither man nor the universe is simply immortal, although we believe that man, as a spirit, can never become ultimately and definitively nothing. The fact that he cannot die, however, may also be a fearful threat. Condemning himself to eternal damnation in "hell", man is also immortal and this is a common theme in Christian teaching.

"Holy immortality" is much more than that. It is a state of holiness, completeness and life in the Spirit of God: a life enjoyed not only by man's soul, but by his body and by everything that he bears within him which is capable of fulfilling his being. It is, in other words, the eternal life of the entire universe. When the Eucharist is celebrated, then, the whle universe is transformed and becomes heaven, present here and now.

Joyful acceptance

Does our prayer as Christians reflect a joyful acceptance of the world? First we must look for the basic meaning of the resurrection. Only if we can find that shall we be able to answer any question. The great difficulty confronting us here is, however that we do not know exactly what the resurrection really is. We can, on the other hand, be quite certain that the resurrection body is the perfect expression of a soul that is eternally united with God. Taking that as our point of departure, we can attempt to define what the resurrection body will *not* be.

It will not, in the first place, suffer. It will be completely absorbed into the spirit, a spirit which will be entirely with God. We know this with certainty because it is a constantly recurring theme in the New Testament in connection with eternal glory. In the Bible, the fact that we shall not suffer after the resurrection is simply the corollary of the fact that we be endlessly given. When we have reached the state of resurrection, our bodies will cease to be alienated from God and will enjoy a direct experience of God. We shall experience God with all our senses. Having said this, let me now digress a little further.

A CHRISTIAN'S "SENSES"

Insofar as it is "Christian", that is, insofar as it expresses faith in the resurrection, prayer can never be hostile to the world or to the body. Ignatius of Loyola described in his "Spiritual Exercises" how man is able inwardly to "feel and taste" God even during his life on earth. According to Ignatius, the application of the senses to God is a stage of mysticism — I would call it the highest stage. The same doctrine can also be found in the writings of many of the great fathers and theologians of the Church, including Origen and Augustine. Augustine, for example, describes how he experienced the proximity of God with his senses in a well-known passage in his *Confessions,* which I would like to quote here because it tells us a great deal about the theme that we are considering.

"What do I love, God, when I love you? Not the beauty of a body or the rhythm of troubled times. Not the splendour of light that is so dear to the eyes, nor the perfume of flowers, balms or spices. Not the melodies in the world of many different sounds. Not the manna and the honey. Not the limbs of love, so delightful in embrace. None of these do I love when I love my God. And yet I love a light and a sound and an aroma and a taste and an embrace when I love my God — the light and sound and aroma and taste and embrace of my inner man. There is a radiation that cannot be contained in any space. . . . There is a sound that cannot be diminished with the passing of time. There is a perfume that cannot be blown away by any wind. There is a taste that cannot be made bitter by satiety. There is a clinging that cannot be broken by weariness. That is what I love when I love my God".

This text can be contrasted with a passage from Origen's works: "The holy prophets discovered the sensuousness of

God. They looked in a divine way and heard in a divine way. They tasted and sensed by means of, if I may speak in this way, a non-sensuous sensuousness and touched the word by faith, so that it flowed over them like healing rain". The experiences described by Augustine, Origen and other Christian authors anticipate the state of the resurrection body, in which everything will be ultimately fulfilled.

ACCEPTANCE

Now that we have considered this question of the senses and their connexion with the risen state, we can approach the question of Christian joy in accepting the world. First of all, however, we must ask, quite simply, what does this joyful acceptance of the world mean in the Christian sense? Christians set themselves the task of following Jesus, who was poor, despised, rejected and finally crucified. The climax of the "Spiritual Exercises" of Ignatius of Loyola is marked by an exposition of the folly of the cross and the same idea is expressed by the author in his "Constitutions": "We should, in love, direct our minds towards this, because it is of great, even decisive importance for our Lord and Creator — the extent to which all growth in the life of the spirit depends on rejecting completely and not simply half everything that passes in the world for love and desire and on accepting, even, with the whole force of the soul, longing for what Christ our Lord loved and took on himself."

Does this reflect a joyful acceptance and affirmation of the world? One thing is quite certain — Ignatius did not accept the world joyfully as though God and the world or time and eternity were harmoniously reconciled in advance. In the same way, we too cannot assent to the world as though man were automatically in it and looking forward to an eventual state of blessedness with God. But why not?

My answer to this is that God is more than the world. He has broken into our existence. In his revelation of himself, he has called us out of the world and into his life. He has subjected everything in the world to a criterion which is not that of the world. He is a God of supernatural grace whose dealings with man are always free and always personal. The ultimate norm for everything that the Christian does is always "God's glory" or, as Ignatius would say, the Divine Majesty. Everything that happens in the world is ultimately dependent on the will of the Lord. The norm is, in the last resort, not man, his desires and aspirations, but only what pleases God.

That is the final justification of the Christian practice of discerning the spirits, which is not a discernment of man's inner impulses on the basis of universal moral norms, but rather a listening to God's word, a seeking for and finding the free commandment given by a personal God to man in whatever situation he finds himself. What is more, since the Christian encounters this God above all in Jesus Christ, he is bound to accept the folly of the cross, which is fundamentally an expression of his readiness to follow this God when he calls him out of himself and into the world.

It is precisely from this kind of attitude, this idea of God and this sort of response of readiness to accept the cross that the Christian grows towards a really joyful affirmation of the world.

I would call possibly only one factor essential to prayer. We are bound to accept the world joyfully and to give our full assent to it, but, because we have given ourselves to the God who lies beyond this world and have submitted ourselves to his will, we are ready to obey his commandments, even when he sends us into the world and tells us to find him in it.

In this context, it is relevant to mention an important concept that has long played a part in the spiritual life. Although this concept of "indifference" did not originate with Ignatius of Loyola, he may well have made his impact on it. In spiritual writings, the word does not have the current, contemporary meaning usually associated with indifference. It points above all to a serene readiness to carry out God's commandments. True Christian piety should therefore always − because of this indifference − have a final reserve or coolness towards all things, because all God's possessions are bound to accept God as greater than all possessions.

It is that kind of attitude that results in the Christian's readiness always to listen to any call from God to undertake new tasks and to go out again and again to new places where God can be found and served. This attitude leads to a willingness to accept new forms of service wherever they may be found and changes in oneself and one's way of life. It also produces a courageous acceptance that no one way is the only way to God − we have to look for God on all the ways of our experience. Through Christian indifference and the attitude that it stimulates, too, we can come to accept the cross, if and when it pleases the Divine Majesty of God. This indifference is, after all, basically a modest and reasonable attitude.

When a Christian joyfully accepts the world, then, he is not being naively optimistic or integrating himself into the world. His joyful affirmation is the consequence of his experience of the one with whom he has become one in the folly of the cross. The Christian who has found the God of the life hereafter will take up his task in the world and continue to carry it out until the Lord comes again.

Although I have attempted to answer many questions connected with the Christian's joyful affirmation of the

world, there remain two which I have so far not considered.
The first is the question of our apostolate in the service of
the Church. The second, which is even more important for
some Christians, is this: how can this kind of spirituality be
practised by lay people?

APOSTOLATE

How are we to assess the new situation in which we, as
members of the Church, have to carry out our apostolate in
the world today?

Being intelligent

The most important Christian duty today is to be intelligent.
This is, of course, no more than a fundamental demand of
Christian faith itself, but we are only now becoming aware of
its full dimensions. To be intelligent as a Christian means to
ask questions, to enter new spheres of knowledge and understanding and to test all the concepts of our faith. The courage
to do this does not indicate a restless longing for novelty; it
points to the virtue of intelligence. This intelligence consists
of an absolute honesty, of an openness to every truth,
wherever it may come from, and of a determined search for
what is right.

As Christians, we are above all looking for the truth. We
are not seeking easy answers. We cannot go back, nor can we
even pause and hesitate. If our general education is in-
complete or if we fail to understand our partner in dialogue,
we shall not carry out our task as Christians. If our aim is to
be apostles of the Church in the modern world, we shall try
to combat intellectual lethargy and mental mediocrity
especially in ourselves and especially here and now. In the
Old Testament, there is an utterance, attributed to God,
which has all the undertones of a threat: "My people are

destroyed for lack of knowledge; because you have rejected knowledge, I reject you" (Hos. 4. 6).

Our idea of God
Our idea of God is going through a process of purification. The Christian today is no longer talking so easily, so confidently and in so matter-of-fact a way about God. He is even going so far as to admit that he does not know and cannot express all the mysteries of God. Man's experience of the transcendence of God is one of the most striking graces of the modern age. We ought to be grateful to atheists for having obliged us to be honest about God and for having put an end to our cheating with the divine reality. The modern Christian can no longer put up with a God who can be measured out, taken for granted and, as it were, tapped on the shoulder like someone with whom we are all too familiar.

Humble attitude of mind
I have noticed that modern man has a very humble attitude of mind. Humility is one of the best characteristics of the world today. Humility expresses a modest love of reality. This realistic attitude also, I believe, characterizes contemporary theology. The present-day theologian is undoubtedly struggling humbly and honestly with the truth in an attempt to express the inexhaustible mystery of God more and more precisely. But, whereas theological systematizations and formulations are transient, faith remains, and only authentic faith that can free us from the temptation of applying to human systems and values those realities which belong only to God. The modern Christian is not in any sense triumphant in his thinking. He is aware of how much he fails, but is also sure that he cannot be proud of his small measure of success. What is needed above all in the Christian apostolate today is less propaganda and more bearing of witness.

Towards the world

The new situation in which Christians are placed is also marked by a new form of holiness that is directed towards the world. The modern saint bears witness to the truth in the order of God's creation and waits, watches and listens attentively to the moment of grace. He finds his task as a Christian wherever it may be in the world.

Free choice

Christianity must be a free choice and the life of faith must be a fundamentally personal event. Christian faith cannot simply be inherited.

Ultimate reasons

An astonishing number of young people today give a great deal of thought to their reasons for deciding about important issues in their lives and refuse to let themselves be driven by unconscious motivation into new situations. They want to know whether, in the way of life that they have freely chosen, they can "save their souls": in other words, whether they can express in their lives a genuine Christian love for their fellow men and thus carry out the task imposed on them by Christ.

New kind of piety

Young people today are also intensely interested in the person of Christ himself. Although Christianity has much to tell us about truth and Christian doctrines are important, the essence of our faith is a living relationship with the historical person, Jesus of Nazareth. Modern man often finds in Christ the authenticity, originality and sincerity that he is so urgently seeking.

A demand

Modern man regards Christianity as a demand. The future belongs to those who respond to this demand and whose goal is almost unattainable. Christianity is not a religion of external miracles. The miraculous element in our faith is to be found above all in ourselves – we are the miracles of Christ.

Decline of clericalism

The decline of clericalism is a feature of contemporary society. The Church's influence on the political life of the state and on society as a whole is certainly declining and in some countries it has almost completely disappeared. In addition to this loss of influence on the world, the laity are less subject to the domination of priests and, in many countries in the West, lay people have become entirely independent and mature. This is completely in accordance with the spirit of Christian teaching, since Christ himself was unequivocal in his rejection of all attempts to exert power over others.

Fellow men

Finally, the modern Christian is convinced that faith is an affirmation of his fellow men. The man who affirms this and commits himself totally to his fellow-men is a Christian, whether he knows it or not. The man who, on the other hand, does not commit himself to his fellow men has failed to grasp the reality of life and faith, whether he is a leading theologian or a lay person who regularly receives the sacrament.

These, then, are a few of the positive signs pointing to the Church's future and especially to the form our apostolate in the world might take.

A LAYMAN'S ACCEPTANCE

But how is the lay person to express this joyful acceptance of the world in his life? I know that my answer may hurt some of my fellow-Christians who are priests, but, in all honesty, I am bound to give it. I do not intend to outline the fundamental characteristics of lay spirituality in the world today in this concluding section, but will do no more than simply point to one aspect of that spirituality. This is based on a passage from the gospel of Mark (6. 1–6) and may throw light on the attitude that the lay person may be expected to have today.

"He went away from there and came to his own country; and his disciples followed him. And on the sabbath he began to teach in the synagogue; and many who heard him were astonished, saying, 'Where did this man get all this? What is the wisdom given to him? What mighty works are wrought by his hands! Is not this the carpenter, the son of Mary, and brother of James and Joseph and Judas and Simon, and are not his sisters here with us?' And they took offence at him. And Jesus said to them, 'A prophet is not without honour, except in his own country, and among his own kin, and in his own house.' And he could do no mighty work there, except that he laid his hands upon a few sick people and healed them. And he marvelled because of their unbelief".

What the people in the synagogue said, in other words, was: "How is it that this man from our own village can talk to us in the name of God? He is only a joiner, after all, and one of us, yet he stands up in our synagogue and thinks that he is better than us. All he can produce is ideology and we don't need that. Surely a joiner should speak about wood and nails, not about man and God. We find it shocking and disturbing to listen to a man like us. We would rather hear a properly appointed preacher, dressed for the part, speak solemnly about sacred matters".

We can, of course, have no real objection to this. It may be necessary, meaningful and even splendid, but only so long as we do not forget that the message that is addressed to us here comes from the very heart of our everyday lives and goes to the heart of our freedom as men to choose. It is only then, when such conditions prevail, that we should be indignant when a lay person proclaims the Christian message. Does he not, after all, share in the priesthood of Christ?

If we do not listen to the voice of the ordinary Christian, then all that we have in fact heard are the words of an ideological superstructure. If, moreover, we do not listen to that voice in the Church, then we will not have heard the inner voice of life itself. On the other hand, if we do not at some time or other hear it, we are bound to ask ourselves whether it is perhaps not the voice of the carpenter of Nazareth and whether he can tell us anything that we have not known for a long time already or that is not simply idle talk.

Faith can be justified in the Christian's conscience, but it can also be endangered when it is exposed to the light of everyday life. An even greater danger threatens faith, however, when we are conscious of an appeal being made to us and then believe only if God's word is brought to us by a competent person such as a priest. The text from Mark points to these dangers and stresses that Jesus was unable to perform any miracles in Nazareth. There is, however, the rather timid addition that "he laid his hands upon a few sick people and cured them", giving us the impression that the evangelist wanted to show us what a difficult demand was being made in this episode.

Will we be able to hear the voice of God and respond to the radical demand that it makes in the depths of our being, even if it comes to us by way of an ordinary Christian, perhaps someone who is unknown to us or who is not very well-educated? Will we hear it then as the word spoken by Jesus himself and lived out in his life, death and resurrection?

Will we hear it even if it is proclaimed by someone whom we do not recognize as competent, such as an ordained priest, but who is perhaps living the truth of the Gospel even more fully and is more able of leading us to God than many priests?

It is, of course, easy enough to say Yes in the abstract to these questions, but can we so easily say Yes when the situation arises in the concrete? Many of us — myself included, perhaps — might well be anxious then. All the same, each one of us, whether he is a priest or a layman, is bound to recognize that he is called to live out the Gospel for others in the joy of the Holy Spirit and, when the time comes, to proclaim it either in his own words or from his own experience.

The word of the Holy Spirit is given to us all, but the Spirit does not give us any easy prescriptions that we simply have to follow. The Holy Spirit confronts us with risk and the need for decision and does not allow us to act on the basis of universal principles such as the law and the letter of the law. The word of the Holy Spirit is in fact a question put to each person — priest and layman, man and woman, child and adult. Every individual is asked whether he has the courage to take a risk and make a personal decision.

Giving oneself to God

In this chapter and the next, I shall speak about two prayers, the first by Ignatius of Loyola and the second by Thomas Aquinas.

Ignatius' prayer concludes his "Spiritual Exercises": "Take to yourself, Lord, and accept all my freedom, my memory, my understanding and my will, all that I have and possess. You gave it to me and to you I give it back. It is all yours. Dispose of it entirely according to your will. Give me your love and grace. That is enough for me." At the end of the "Exercises" is a section entitled "Reflection on the Acquisition of Love", which includes the prayer I have just quoted. This section forms a climax to the whole book, and the prayer itself is a summary of all the ideas and resolutions contained in the "Exercises", and is a valuable compendium of prayer in itself.

IGNATIAN PRAYER
A Christian who has completed the "Exercises" is, according to Ignatius, a "lover". Love is a Christian's basic attitude towards reality. In his book, Ignatius sets himself the task, among other things, of defining what love really is, on the

basis of three fundamental concepts: action, communication and service.

Ignatius says of action: "Love must be placed more in works than in words". In Ignatius' opinion, love is related to "work" or action. Love must be able to express itself in the world and not simply in fine words. It must have its own object, a person. The loved being has, as it were, to be created again and again and to be protected both against itself and against the world by the one who loves, who will allow this personal object of his love to live and grow. Love is a selfless activity.

With regard to communication, Ignatius says: "Love consists of mutual communication. This means that the lover gives and communicates to the loved one all that he has and the loved one does the same". In this way, love creates a unity of being. The act of love establishes unity between two otherwise separate beings. I become more completely myself as I experience myself more and more completely as the centre of total consent to being together with others in loving communication with them. Love, then, is communicating, sharing and being with others.

Finally, Ignatius says of service: "Here I ought to pray for an inner knowledge of the great blessings that I have received from God so that I shall be able to serve his Divine Majesty with a thankful mind in all things". Love is therefore essentially a service. Love is our experience of how others are fed by our life-blood and of how they are able to grow, flourish and bear fruit, drawing sustinence from our being.

LOVE

Ignatius puts forward four aspects of God's being and activity and suggests that we should reflect about them and base our lives on them.

The first point in Ignatius' reflection is that God gives. God's love is above all giving, and Ignatius stresses that we should bear in mind that God is not simply the one who loves. He is love. Everything that he is and does is ultimately founded in this love. His giving is therefore as irreducible as his love. Ignatius also insists that God has nothing, because he is everything. This means that he can give nothing but himself. Our task as believers is to assimilate this essential structure of God's being into our own finite being, which means, in the concrete, that I must give myself entirely. I must give myself without depending on the answer that may be given in return by the object of my love and I must above all give *myself*. I have to act in such a way that I am always present in the giving and that I always give something more from the depths of my own being. If I give myself entirely and give *myself*, then I shall be living God's love in my own human love.

The second point is that God is inherent. Ignatius here outlines the order of creation from the earliest and simplest elements created by God to the creation of man. He claims that creation becomes more powerful as God becomes more present in the world. The aim of this part of the reflection is to reveal the God who is inherent in his creation as the ultimate basis of that creation. Ignatius also regards the order of God's grace as the highest point of evolution in the natural world. It is by living, feeling and thinking that we, as creatures, live God's life in a mysterious way.

God is so great, Ignatius teaches, that he has no need to force himself upon us or to place himself in the centre of the universe. His presence in the world is so great and yet at the same time so reserved that we can only become slowly aware of it through constant prayer and often as the result of considerable exertion. Our task is to express the tenderness of God's presence in the creation in which he is inherent in our love. But that means that when we share in the life of another, we must receive into our own life his life, his feelings and his joy. We must take his individual existence, because it is only by receiving that we can really love.

The third aspect of God that Ignatius discusses in his reflection is that God exerts himself. He comes and goes, prepares for his coming, preaches, becomes tired, experiences human anxiety, is nailed to the cross, appears again to men in various forms and sends his Spirit. He never overwhelms us with his divine power. He exerts himself, as Ignatius says in his simple, yet splendid language, for us in the elements, the plants, fruits and animals of creation, in those people who understand us and show us friendship and in so much else besides. The living God is as he appeared to us in Christ. He exerts himself for us, he is troubled and anxious on our behalf and he looks for us everywhere. In all this, he is also a God whom we must, as lovers, learn to resemble. Being concerned is very often the way in which God expresses his love for us and our human concern is therefore God's concern. God wants his humble attitude of service and love to be expressed in our attitudes and actions. We are doing his will if we allow the suffering of others to flow into our being and the fate of the world to become our own fate.

In the fourth place, Ignatius speaks of God's descent. God, who is all-powerful, is nonetheless always ready to descend into the small and lowly sphere of his creation and, of course, the outstanding example of this is his descent into the being of an unknown man from Nazareth.

How do we imitate that attitude? Ignatius believed that we can do it by leading good, pious, just and merciful lives. We can, however, only do this if our whole existence is rooted in God. Ignatius claims that it is only the man who lives in this way who can make the most precious aspect of

the human reality shine out in the confusion of this world —
justice. Only such a man can make the cold world glow with
goodness and only he can live humbly in the presence of the
Absolute in a self-satisfied world and be truly pious. Only
such a man too can, at all levels of his life, maintain an
attitude of genuine sympathy with his fellow men, an
attitude of mercy. Finally, Ignatius insists, all this can only
come about in our lives if we pray in all humility for it.

Anyone making the "Spiritual Exercises" should say
Ignatius' prayer with a great sense of urgency and a determination to give himself after considering each of the four
points in the above reflection.

TAKE AND ACCEPT

Take to yourself, Lord

These words express man's complete gift of himself to God.
The man who says those words sincerely is saying: My God,
you can take everything away from me again. You can, if you
wish, reduce my ability to do anything, deprive me of my
faculties, even destroy my life itself. If this is your desire,
know that you need not consider me at all, since I already
give my consent to it in advance. I agree to anything that you
want to do with me. On the other hand, if, for one reason or
another, it should please you to allow me to continue to live,
then I give you complete control over me — take me and
accept me and all that I have. Use me when, where and how
it pleases you to use me. Let nothing continue to exist in me
that is contrary to your will. Your will be done, in my life.

All my freedom

This act of self-giving is fundamental, because freedom is the
very essence of man's existence. It is freedom that holds the

whole man together and makes him what he really is — a person who is in control of himself. A man is free when his actions flow from the whole of his person. In giving his freedom to God, man gives the central and innermost reality of his life. He gives to God what makes him this particular person with these particular qualities, these experiences in life and this possible future. In giving himself and his freedom in this way, he is saying to God: If it is your will, I will become completely different. I will have entirely different hopes. I will, if necessary, totally eliminate a part of my existence. I will love those and serve those to whom you send me, whoever they may be. I may not be able to remain myself in this, but what does it matter? All that really matters is that you should have complete control over me and my world.

My memory, my understanding and my will

As for my memory, I want to to remember nothing in my life apart from you. I want to reject all the disturbing memories of the past that eat away at my existence. I will be like a newly born child and have no past. If I have a past, it will be you alone. I also give you all my understanding and want to know only what you want me to understand. I will not allow myself to be influenced by systems, partisan views or considerations which can be used for my own advantage. I will seek above all knowledge of you and of your creatures, so that I can look into the things of the world and into men's hearts and not judge by appearances or be swayed by positions of power. What is more, I will only desire what you desire from the world. In the future, all that will happen in my life will be what takes the world towards a greater hope, the promise of your grace. In my will, the world will be set free to move towards its eternal fulfilment, towards you.

All that I have and possess
The word "have" points to ourselves and more strictly to our inner wealth. "Possess", on the other hand, points to the things outside ourselves which protect us against the world, nourish and sustain us. Ignatius is saying here that we should be without anxiety and carefree in our attitude as we go forward to meet the one who is so much greater than us and that we should never let ourselves become enslaved to anything either within ourselves or outside us in the world. The only bonds that we should accept are those which God wants to place on us. We should free ourselves from all those which prevent us from achieving the task that Christ has set us.

You gave it to me and to you I give it back. It is all yours. Dispose of it entirely according to your will
Here, the creature gives something to his God and Creator. It is an incredible aspect of the Christian faith that it is possible for us to do this. God is, after all, everything, and everything, the universe itself, belongs to him. He is, in Paul's words, "all in all". Yet he allows us to give him something. It is important to understand in this context that it is only in giving that man really becomes himself. It is only in giving that he comes to see that he still "has" something and that he *is* something. The man who has never given anything cannot have found himself, his own inner being. On the other hand, the man who gives himself to the infinite God will himself become infinite, so long as the infinite God accepts his finite gift. It is therefore true to say that the man who gives himself to God will receive God's life, which is infinite happiness. By giving ourselves to him, we bear his life in us.

Give me your love and grace. That is enough for me
Apart from God's love and grace, everything is ultimately of secondary importance — all the movements of our heart,

our emotions, our inner wealth, our external possessions, our experiences, our successes and failures and even our very lives. The man who grasps this is really free and can say yes to everything and above all to everything that is good and beautiful. He will love infinitely because he is infinitely loved.

The Christian can never be satisfied with what is finite. Only what is infinite is ultimately enough for him, but it must be loved by him, even if it is small and insignificant when it appears in the world. "Give me your grace" therefore means: give me your grace so that I shall no longer be tied to the external realities of the world, but will be able to see your face everywhere, meet you in every creature and receive you wherever you come forward to meet me. The man who gives himself to God in this way will never reject anyone again, because he knows that God may come to him in any one of his creatures. In acknowledging his absolute need to be given God's love, the Christian opens his whole life to the world, because he is already open to receive God's grace.

In speaking to God in this way with the whole strength of his being, asking him for his love and grace and telling him that it is enough, the believer can at the same time receive not only all the beauty of the world, but also all its cares. What he receives in this way will not prevent him from being completely and exclusively devoted to God. This is because he knows that he can best serve the world by losing himself totally in God and best serve this God by giving entirely to his creatures and receiving all their suffering and all their joy. If he persists in this attitude and lives accordingly, he will gradually come to embrace the whole of mankind and indeed all creation in its obscure and often painful hope of fulfilment in his vision. He will, in a word, come to see God in everything that exists. He will also be able to give himself to the whole of existence because his discovery of the invisible God in what is visible will strengthen him in his task of sustaining the world.

MAGNANIMOUS TOWARDS GOD

Giving oneself to God is intimately connected with every aspect of a man's inner attitude and no one would deny that it is fundamental to Christianity. As we know, God is exalted above the world. He is absolute. He is Spirit and supreme, the great reality that lies behind the world's phenomena. He is independent and holy. Man, on the other hand, is nothing in the presence of God, who lives in inaccessible light. There is an infinite distance between God and man, his creature. They are separated by a wide and deep ravine and man looks into this abyss and his soul is gripped with awe.

Although man's longing cannot be united with the exalted character of God, man longs to and indeed can be connected with the holiness of God and, in achieving this connexion, he himself becomes holy. The link between God and man in holiness can be strengthened more and more until it is perfected in man's vision of God in heaven.

Though exalted far above him, God is not simply separated from man, his creature. He is also very near to him. God's transcendence is intimately connected with his immanence. God is the ultimate ground of the creature's existence and his ultimate goal. He is also, through man, the end to which the whole universe is directed. The creature's life belongs to God and to God alone. God is man's point of departure and his end point.

We as Christians should be above all conscious of our dependence on God. That means *awe*. In awe, we are on the one hand drawn towards God and, on the other, repelled from him. If we have this attitude of dependence and awe, we shall always seek God in his creatures. We shall become more and more orientated towards God.

God is the ground of our being, our point of departure and our end point. We should serve him faithfully in adoration. We have to subordinate our will to the eternal will of God. The essence of all prayer is to bring about in the one praying a decision for God.

"Take to yourself, Lord, and accept" — these words contain the nucleus of Ignatius' prayer. They throw light on the inner attitude of the Christian. I give away everything and I give it to you, Lord. With all my strength and all my capacity, I stand before you. If there is one fibre of my being which does not belong to you, I cut it out.

What should I give?

But what should I give? I should give my free, personal being as a man and my inner wealth, all that I possess in myself. What should my attitude be when I give? A possible answer is that I should give, conscious that I have my origin in him and that I shall return to him. I give everything back to God who is the end point of my life. The Christian who has this attitude places himself entirely at God's disposal and allows God to do what he wants with him. God can exalt him without any danger of pride or self-love secretly undermining his attitude and he will, at the end, be able to say in all sincerity: "Give me your love and grace. That is enough for me".

What takes place between this taking and this giving is Christian holiness. In his gradual movement towards God, the Christian finds rest. He is able to say: "The past is over and done with. My whole future is secure in God."

If we look at Ignatius' prayer in this light, we are inevitably brought back to the ideas expressed in the author's "Reflection on the Acquisition of Love", in which he insists that everything that surrounds us in this life is the result of God's beneficial activity in us. He is, Ignatius emphasizes, present in our souls in everything that we do or aim to do and in all our thoughts. He is the mysterious ground from which streams of light proceed and to which we, who have been caught up in them, return.

Let us apply Ignatius' prayer to the practical Christian life. What are the most important aspects of that life according to this prayer? The Christian must above all give himself entirely and whatever is of less importance must be set aside: "If anyone comes to me and does not hate his own father and mother and wife and children and brothers and sisters, yes, even his own life, he cannot be my disciple" (Luke 14. 26). Nothing must be kept back — everything must be given to God. When this happens, God can occupy the Christian's soul and fill it with light: "But one thing I do, forgetting what lies behind and straining forward to what lies ahead" (Phil. 3. 13). In giving himself totally, man leaves himself and the centre of his little individual person so that God can take up his habitation in him: "I have been crucified with Christ; it is no longer I who live, but Christ who lives in me" (Gal. 2. 20).

Human fulfilment

Jesus's missionary activity begins with the proclamation of the nearness of heaven. He has promised man that he will be fulfilled and that that fulfilment is near. That definitive fulfilment is open to all men. Whether they do it consciously or unconsciously, all men are capable of contemplation, which is a fundamental characteristic of human existence. Wherever that contemplation takes place, Christianity is present, even though it may be manifested in a strange or imperfect form. This is because Christ himself has implanted a tension in man's soul which results in prayer.

CHRISTIAN CONTEMPLATION
The contemplative process is more than simply — establishing and verifying data. It does not include any attempt to categorize the object of contemplation within the framework of our empirical experience of the world. It is an immersion into that experience, which is sought for its own sake.

Contemplation originates in man's giving of himself. What he contemplates and experiences is related to nothing but itself. It is a place of direct encounter. The ability to contemplate in this way is certainly not part of everyone's everyday experience and indeed it is nowadays a very rare gift, which would seem to be becoming even rarer, at least in its authentic form. We talk too much and, although this may not be in itself disastrous, it has the effect of diminishing our ability to contemplate because it almost always takes place outside the sphere of contemplation. We do not dwell long enough on any object.

Contemplation is also a higher form of knowledge. What is contemplated cannot be proved by empirical means. In contemplation, there is a need to move consciously away from purely sensory perception. Contemplative man has to break out of the illusory world and of the caricature of reality that is inherent in this illusion. He strives to leave the world that has already been interpreted for him and presses forward to achieve direct union with his fellow men, the world and God. Above all, however, he is bound to recognise that he does not possess what he is contemplating and that, although he is entirely without security, he is never uncertain.

Thirdly, contemplation is not a process of bringing individual experiences slowly together. It can prove nothing. What man can experience in contemplation, however, is that there may be an element of fulfilment even in the least significant of things. There is no security in the sphere of contemplation. At first sight, the world often seems ambiguous. A Christian contemplative, however, can learn to go beyond this duality and see the meaningful unity underlying the world.

NEARNESS OF HEAVEN

In the New Testament, human fulfilment is given the name of newness. What this newness is cannot be expressed directly. It is described in images in the fourth Gospel, although the author stresses what has already been said by Paul: "What no eye has seen, nor ear heard, nor the heart of man conceived, what God has prepared for those who love him" (1 Cor. 2. 9).

Heaven is so near that we are often unable to see it. As Paul said: "If anyone is in Christ, he is a new creation" (2 Cor. 5. 17). The Christian is called to live in this tension – he is already in heaven, but his experience of this heaven is still to come.

Thomas Aquinas expressed the nearness of this heaven in man's life and experience on earth in his "prayer for contemplation, which he himself said, inwardly contemplating". But how was Thomas able to express man's ultimate fulfilment in his prayer?

PRAYER OF THOMAS AQUINAS

There is a prayer in which Thomas Aquinas expressed his experience of heaven and outlined the structure of man's fulfilment and the substance of Christian contemplation: "Give to my body, you who are the fulness of giving, the beauty of clarity, a readiness to act, a capacity for fineness and strength to be free from suffering".

A universal human longing is expressed in this prayer, in which the temporary nature of man's existence recedes before his movement towards ultimate and permanent fulfilment. The prayer shows man projecting himself forward into a state in which everything is clear and he is at the point to which his longing is leading him. In this clear state of existence, his whole life is fine and he no longer suffers. It is a state of infinite and lasting joy.

The beauty of clarity, a readiness to act, a capacity for fineness and strength to be free from suffering – in a word, heaven. That is the goal towards which every contemplative Christian strives, but not only every Christian, since it is true to say that all men, whether they explicitly confess to faith in God or not, long secretly for this final state.

Fulness of giving

Thomas Aquinas' experience of heaven does not have an intellectual origin. It arises as the result of prayer, indeed of asking. The opening word of the prayer tells us this: "give". The transfigured world is already present in the longing experienced by the poor who beseech God. We have to suffer poverty and impotence if we are to experience what God's promise really means. Where, then, is God experienced as a person in the fulness of his being? This personal encounter takes place, I believe, when all man's earthly hopes break down and he finds himself at the ultimate limit of his existence. It is there that he begins to beseech God, whom he experiences as the one who is totally different.

Of course, God is also present in beauty, radiance and blessing. Very often, however, God appears most powerfully as the fulness of giving when man is suffering from a deep sense of his own utter impotence and when he has reached the furthest limit of his life, which he seems to be living in vain. At such times of poverty, man experiences an irresistible need to implore God.

It is also perhaps true to say that, when man prays in this sense at the ultimate limit of his existence, he is in the last resort simply accepting and giving his assent to his own impotence. This basic prayer affirming the impotence of man's life is expressed, in the concrete, in the form of adoration, praise, thanksgiving and petition. In this sense too, prayer is an event which embraces the whole of man's existence. Man prays in this way when he is no longer intent on dominating his fellow men and when he fully accepts that he is in himself capable of nothing and is exposed to every approach of love and friendship. Then, he prays with this sickness of the soul, with his whole body and with the often tedious carrying out of his everyday tasks. He prays whenever he becomes conscious of the presence in himself of a deep existential sadness clinging to everything that he does. He lives, in prayer, in a frontier situation.

He is not able to acquire this attitude of prayer for himself – it can only be given by God. God has no reason or motive for giving his presence in this way or for giving man the opportunity of going to his ultimate limit and being able, from that point, to enter completely the state of loneliness. God also gives us all death. It is possible for man to plunge into insignificance at death and it is also prayer not to do this, but to continue to bear with God and allow oneself to be humbled by him. If we do this, God will, as it were, reward us by leading us into an even darker night of silence. There are as many different ways of depriving man's existence of its power as there are different varieties of human destiny.

The fulness of God's giving is so great that each individual man can be given his own way into the state of loneliness. Christ experienced this loneliness and both the infinite fulness of absolute existence and the unique human fate of finite individuality were revealed in him.

Give to my body

Aquinas speaks of the body in connexion with his petition for the gift of God's presence. He is asking not only for immortality, but also for the resurrection of the body. There is a clear reference here to the traditional Christian teaching about the human body and its fulfilment. Christianity has always seen man's fulfilment in terms of the resurrection, the word standing, in this context certainly, as a cipher pointing to what cannot be explained. Man's bodily nature becomes personal at the resurrection, when man enters the presence of God and is brought to life at death.

Man is fulfilled in his resurrection, which takes place immediately in death. Until recently, it has been usual to think of death as the time when the soul is separated from the body, but this understanding of death is unsatisfactory. Man is not composed of two distinct elements, body and soul; he is a single being, in whom matter and spirit are indissolubly united. His body is the visible unfolding of his soul and his soul is that aspect of his being which must, of necessity, proceed from the urge of matter. This is why death, which is the moment when man is at the point of transition towards fulfilment, has to be understood as resurrection.

We may, however, go further and say that man's resurrection includes every aspect of the universe. The world is as it were concentrated in man and is truly expressed in his body, which is united with his spirit. The world is not simply the space in which man develops, however, but belongs essentially to the unity of body and soul which is so clearly manifested in man. If man's soul is immortal, it must therefore experience resurrection. In the same way, the resurrection of the body must be the transfiguration of the universe. The whole of the world enters fulfilment with man.

Beauty of clarity
Even in his experience on this earth, man is already moving towards the infinite. This experience which lies beyond the limits of the finite world is known as "heaven". Heaven is the depths of human experience present within us while we are still on earth in the form of longing. The fundamental urge of the universe which, over hundreds of millions of years, has become transformed into life is, as it were, concen-

trated in our human existence and has finally achieved spiritual consciousness in man. Heaven is at the point where all our longings converge. God is that beauty which is ever old and ever new.

Readiness to act

Man is above all longing. There is in him a mysterious quality which drives him constantly further to action. He can never rest. Human life can only be fulfilled and man can only be born as man when his longing for what cannot be reached is accomplished in his existence. When that happens, man's real birth will have taken place. Heaven is the necessary existential demand made by man. It is, however, always given to him in grace.

Man also looks forward to the Absolute in his knowledge. He discovers different laws and complicated interrelationships. At the same time, however, he has a presentiment of something greater than himself. Every expression of human knowledge contains a consciousness of God as the one who is completely different.

Capacity for fineness

Man did not choose his actual presence. He can never entirely overcome his strangeness. His soul is spirit which has become body and it is only when he leaves his present narrowness, both body and soul, that he will be able to live free and unconstrained. That is the state of heaven which man senses, while he is here on earth, in the form of an eternal longing.

Free from suffering

Despite his consciousness of his own impotence, man is turned entirely outwards towards the universe around him. He never ceases to try, throughout the whole of his life on earth, to conquer the world and is aware of his power to control and fashion nature. On the other hand, he is equally aware of his limitations, and confronted with his own failure, his gradual self-destruction.

Taking place at the same time as this destruction of the outer man is the creation of the inner man, a continuous process by which man's narrow, limited and finite existence on earth is able to move towards the infinite. A man, we may say, is born and, in his life, learns to accept, through trusting in God, that this life will eventually reach a point of collapse. He achieves very little in life, but his failure teaches him that there must be a heaven. In his love, friendship and joy, he tries to communicate this hope of heaven to others. The time comes when he must die and afterwards people say: "He has passed away. None of us will see him again". He, however, experiences the final, definitive security of heaven, when he has been received into the person of God himself.

Providence

Providence is one of the most important words in the Christian vocabulary, but it is not immediately understood nowadays. It is not one of those terms which clearly reflect the religious experience of modern man. A search in the Bible will at once reveal a number of key-terms — for example, brother, love of one's neighbour and future — each of which opens a door to our understanding of grace and the Christian message, but providence is not among them. Yet it is undeniably a concept which can provide us with indispensable information about the finite nature of man at prayer and the infinite goodness of God.

ESSENCE OF PROVIDENCE

Modern man is opposed to every form of injustice. He would certainly regard as unjust a divine providence that was interpreted within the framework of a "magical" view of the world, because man has always tried to persuade and even force God by magic means to do what he wanted. The Christian attitude is quite different — man should be subject to God's power.

If divine providence were simply a means of making God available to us so that we could use his power in our everyday lives — if it were a form of magic — then we could only conclude that it was no more than an expression of our baser, self-seeking nature. God himself condemned this concept of providence, above all in the Book of Job. Christian teaching too could never contain a sentence like "The man who enjoys prosperity is a better man". The very opposite is so often true — there are men who are entirely dedicated to God and whose lives are quite unsuccessful and full of misfortune and suffering, men who always seem to be where the lightning strikes. The message of God's providence is one of God's most profound truths and above all a proclamation of joy and liberation made to God's closest friends, in other words, to the poor and oppressed. What this message conveys to us is, in the last resort: If you have no one to help you and can see no way out, think of God, who is always with you and will always stand up for you.

We are bound to ask whether the message of God's providence is not basically the same as Paul's "hoping against hope", as expressed in his letter to the Christians at Rome: "In hope he (Abraham) believed against hope" (Rom. 4. 18). Those who are God's favourites are the very people who suffer misfortune, precisely because they would have no hope without God. In this sense, then, providence consists of a "change of heart". God does not intervene in a miraculous way in our lives, do away with all that threatens us, or overcome all attacks against us. On the contrary, providence means that there is a final way out. Everything may stay as it was. There may be no outward change. We may continue to be threatened. We may have to go on living with our anxiety and our fear. But everything has changed inwardly, because in and through everything God's goodness has appeared. Man can now say: It is painful, but in the end it does not matter.

It cannot, of course, be disputed that there is, in the Old

Testament especially, a surface current which would seem to flow in the opposite direction to this idea of divine providence. The pious are often promised success, victory over their enemies, prosperity and security. At the same time, however, there is always an undercurrent which reveals Israel's expectation of something quite different. The prophetic books and the Wisdom literature above all proclaim God's consolation of his people in their suffering and speak of their firm hope in a way out of their oppression. The Second Isaiah, for example, makes God cry out: "Fear not, for I have redeemed you; I have called you by name, you are mine" (Is. 43. 1) and: "You are precious in my eyes, and honoured, and I love you" (Is. 43. 4). The psalmist sings: "The Lord is my light and my salvation; whom shall I fear? The Lord is the stronghold of my life; of whom shall I be afraid?" (Ps. 27. 1). In the Book of Proverbs, we read: "If you sit down, you will not be afraid; when you lie down, your sleep will be sweet. Do not be afraid of sudden panic" (Prov. 3. 24–25) and in another psalm: "Even though I walk through the valley of the shadow of death, I fear no evil, for thou art with me" (Ps. 23. 4). These promises made by God to Israel point to an entirely new dimension in man's understanding of faith – the serene recollectedness that he experiences when, in his distress, he trusts in God.

If we are to understand the biblical concept of God's providence correctly, we must recognize that God put his people to the most severe of tests and never prevented them from being struck by the blows of fate. He required them, moreover, to remain calm in times of extreme distress, as though he were assuring them that the aspect of their lives which was ultimately most important of all would never be taken from them, because that was eternally in his keeping. Even if everything were to break down around and within them, his promise of heaven would remain.

Man's joy over the inner freedom brought to him by Christ and his confident trust in God's power is even more strongly expressed in the New Testament. Perhaps the most concise and at the same time most striking expression of the Christian understanding of God's providence can be found in Paul's text: "Who shall separate us from the love of Christ? Shall tribulation, or distress, or persecution, or famine, or nakedness, or peril, or sword? . . . I am sure that neither death, nor life, nor angels, nor principalities, nor things present, nor things to come, nor powers, nor height, nor depth, nor anything else in all creation, will be able to separate us from the love of God in Christ Jesus our Lord" (Rom. 8. 35–39). The power of God's grace will, in the end, overcome all the powers of the world, all external threats, all psychological difficulties and all expressions of human sinfulness.

As Christians we should be able to trust with unwavering confidence in God and his ultimate salvation. We can confidently hope despite all that we experience in this world, for all these experiences pass and God remains for ever. Paul penetrates deeply into the mystery of God's providence: "We know that in everything God works for good with those who love him" (Rom. 8. 28), a statement which stands directly in the context of Christian revelation and to which Augustine added, quite logically, in his commentary: "also sins".

In the last resort what we are at present and what may happen to us in the future are not of fundamental importance, since God's faithfulness and mercy transcend everything, including man's guilt and its consequences. God's omnipresence and transcendence give an entirely new meaning to our lives and can act as a further step towards God. In Jesus God's mercy appeared in our midst and the promise was made present: "Behold, I have set before you an open door, which no one is able to shut" (Apoc. 5. 8).

The message of providence is basically a proclamation of the resurrection of Christ. The apostles experienced the death of their leader, a man who radiated goodness and a spirit of human understanding during his life on earth. He was able to remain uninfluenced by the powers of this world, and was clearly on the side of the weak and the oppressed. He was a simple man, whose greatness consisted in the fact that he entered into the experiences that cramp our lives and make them difficult. He hated no one, always had a good word to say on behalf of his friends, and never "returned evil for evil" (1 Pet. 3. 9). Yet this man was put to death.

This man, Jesus of Nazareth, became the very essence of genuine humanity by virtue of his attitude while he was still on earth and, ever since his life, death and resurrection, every human being who lives his life honestly and authentically in the attitude of Christ himself not only makes Christ present but is fundamentally a Christian, whether he explicitly confesses Christ as Lord or not. There is no longer any power in the world which can take Christ from us.

FALSE IDEAS

The Christian message of God's providence is at the very heart of our faith and prayer, since everything that Christ has proclaimed to us comes together in this message. It is important to know precisely what is implied in it. Our understanding of providence generally has tended to become secular, and falsified. The Christian teaching has to be carefully distinguished from other ideas about providence which seem to be very close, but are essentially different. I will limit myself to two of this ideas, since all the others can, in my opinion, ultimately be traced back to these.

The word "providence" is frequently used nowadays to

denote something fundamentally mythological. Even many Christians believe that there is a supreme being who watches over them and makes sure that everything will be all right in their lives. This is not in itself a wrong notion, but it is frequently linked with the idea of good fortune and then it easily slips into a mythological understanding of providence which is almost synonymous with good luck. This mythological view of God's providence is not the ultimate falsification, however, for at the lowest level of all, our understanding of divine providence can be pure superstition. The obvious example of this is to be found in the popularity of horoscopes, fortune-telling and predictions of the future which are almost always happy. No Christian can ever believe that these phenomena have anything to do with the Christian teaching about God's providence.

My second example of a false concept of providence can be defined briefly as a view of divine providence based on order in the world. Values such as goodness and truth have to be protected against external forces and this sometimes results in the man who regards these values as particularly significant attributing a "sacral" character to this world-order. One consequence of this is that such a person may come to regard himself as enjoying a special understanding of the way in which the world is ordered and as being in intimate communion with the underlying reality of the universe. Such an attitude has nothing to do with the Christian view of providence.

Both these attitudes towards providence are characterized by a special attitude towards the world. Neither view has anything at all to do with Christian faith. Both are basically reflections of a fairy-tale attitude towards reality. The Christian attitude is quite different: neither inwardly nor outwardly are we at the mercy of powers and dominions;

we are called to accept our freedom and use it to control our destiny.

What is the fundamental meaning of providence and its connexion with change, and what is it that changes? Providence is something that happens in man. A man who believes in providence has to change his manner of thinking. Indeed, providence consists ultimately of this *metanoia*, or change of attitude within a man. His destiny may not undergo any change at all, but it is given an entirely new meaning. God does not, after all, play with the world. He created it and watches over it as creator, but, if we look at the world from the point of view of his providence, nothing really changes in it. On the other hand, however, everything in it is transformed. Our view of God, the world and our fellow men is entirely transformed.

OUR VIEW OF GOD

God becomes the fundamental question of our personal destiny when this transformation takes place. He becomes the God of our life, the God who wants to say something personal, something that deeply concerns us. Who, then, is this God, the God of our experience of life? There is little doubt that his nature cannot be expressed in formulae, concepts or systematic definitions. What is the essential aspect of our destiny in life? In considering this question, we have to bear in mind, that mankind's great image of God is bound to emerge gradually from our fragmentary and much smaller experiences of him.

What Christ preached first of all was the message that God is very close indeed to man. That message made many who heard it hostile towards him, because it called on men to be truly human in their relationship with God. At the same time it expressed a protest against a purely literal interpretation of the law, in which the God of man's personal experience was absent. It was also a protest against all hypocrisy and insincerity in religious experience. Jesus was the friend of all tax-collectors and prostitutes who were truthful in their examination of themselves and were looking timidly for God. He was less well-received by those who considered themselves to be just. Christ spoke directly to people in their whole existence, challenging them individually and collectively as the community which we call the Church. Wherever the God of our life, who is very close to us, is experienced, we become aware of a new direction in our existence. This God embraces our fear and despair and overcomes them and enables us to know with certainty that, despite our hesitations and wavering, we have a firm foothold. Our direct experience of God's immanence makes us confident, despite our many deviations and mistakes, that we are sustained by one whom we can trust utterly. We know where we come from, where we are and where we are going. We know a little of the inner mystery of our existence.

When we are overwhelmed by the presence of God in our lives, we lose the fanatical enthusiasm that we may have for the world and at the same time, in becoming more human, become more able to humanize the world. We lose our sense of dependence on fate existing inside and outside us and become much more fundamentally open to God. The attitude of a Christian with regard to God is always one of openness to life and to the truth.

The Christian can always be aware of the fact that his guilt will be forgiven and that a new way will always be made open to him. There will always be sufficient light for him to be able to see ahead for the next few steps. That is God's promise: it is not much, but it is enough. Throughout history, men have lived in the light of this promise and with this attitude towards God. We too should pray to be counted among those magnificent people, and not try to make God greater by making the world and our fellow men smaller.

OUR VIEW OF THE WORLD

Each of the things and events of which our world consists is related to an individual member of human society. Each of us selects from what is available to him whatever is most suitable to him as an individual. In this way, he reduces the world with which he is associated to his own particular world.

Things are bound to appear in a different light for the Christian, however, who believes that the ultimate reality, the new man, is not yet seen. The world as we know it is not a definitive reality, but is rather something that exists and develops because of God's continued creative work and man's attitude of co-operation in God's creation. It is fundamentally orientated towards the continued existence of men as sons of God, whose purpose is that man should be holy in this world. This holy state can, however, only come about with the free consent of man. If man prevents this freedom from being expressed, he will restrict the action of God himself. If, on the other hand, he allows his freedom to remain open, he will let God's will be freely and openly expressed.

Our faith is severely tested if God's promise is apparently not fulfilled. We can say with certainty, however, that God's promise and its fulfilment are closely linked to our search for the kingdom of God and his justice. The person seeking an answer to the problem of the fulfilment of God's promise in the world must first question his own conscience. We must, however, always bear in mind, when considering this question, that man cannot ultimately provide a complete explanation for the meaning of God's providence.

The ultimate inability of man to answer the question "what is providence?" is partly attributable to the fact that it is a reality which always points to the future. The fundamental meaning of God's providence is not to be found in man's spiritual or physical well-being in the present world, but in the conviction that the kingdom of God will come, that his justice will be fulfilled, and that man and the whole of creation will be made new.

That conviction throws a good deal of light on the Christian practice of praying for others. We very often experience a sense of impotence with regard to the distress suffered by our fellow men. We stand by helpless while a friend is threatened by a disastrous combination of events in the world and, motivated by love, spontaneously call on God to avert the threat. At the same time, however, we know that it would be unworthy of a Christian to expect his God to be concerned purely with man's well-being here and now on this earth, so we leave it to God to grant the petition in whatever way he will. What we in fact say in this prayer is: "I ask you, God, to let this person for whom I am praying experience you as the God of love and as a safe refuge. Let this experience be stronger than all the distress which threatens to overwhelm him at present and which may assail him in the future. Let him really experience your love as a force that will overcome his own sense of hopelessness".

God is joy
The ultimate meaning of this reflection and indeed of all the meditations in this book can be summed up in one word — joy. The joyful man is already on his way towards an encounter with Christ. As Ignatius of Loyola says: "Only God, our Lord, can, without any previous motive, give consolation to the soul, since it is left exclusively to the Creator

to enter the soul, to leave it and to move it in such a way that it can be drawn entirely into the love of his Divine Majesty. Without any motive means without previous feeling or knowledge of any object which might bring about a consolation of this kind in the soul by means of acts of the understanding or the will". If you feel really free and are convinced that life is good and worth living, if you have ceased to feel in any way oppressed, and if you can receive and give life with every breath you take, then God is active within you and you have really experienced him and his love.

God is joy. Whatever deeply troubles us and darkens our lives is certainly not God, since God only gives himself to his friends. The man who tries to banish joy from his life is not only against Christianity but against Christ himself. He is against the Christ who appeared in the glory of his resurrection and said: "It is I — do not be afraid".

Conclusion

Since Christ became man, God has no other face than that of our neighbour. The confusion in the world today regarding belief and unbelief and the immense range of attitudes towards life and of views of God and man can be simplified as a division of mankind into two opposing camps. On the one hand are those who are concerned with themselves and their own advancement and, on the other, those who try to serve their fellow men.

This division runs through the whole of human society and through each individual. Every man can say (if he is honest with himself): Each of these two camps is present in me. In the end, the social, political or cultural level at which each of us lives is really not important. Some of these levels are not of our choosing and, in the case of others, it is hardly possible to judge why a man chooses to live at a certain level or even at what level he is living at a given moment. What is important is that any man can serve his neighbour and, if he chooses to do this, he is experiencing God and his love, whether he is able to give a name to that unfathomable mystery or not.

This idea is very important. It is at the heart of the Christian message and must therefore be at the heart of our prayer.